Freedom
of Speech

POINT
COUNTERPOINT

Freedom of Speech

Alan Allport

SERIES CONSULTING EDITOR
Alan Marzilli, M.A., J.D.

CHELSEA HOUSE
PUBLISHERS
A Haights Cross Communications Company

Philadelphia

This book is intended to serve only as a general introduction to the political and legal issues surrounding the freedom of speech. It is not intended as legal advice. If you have a legal problem, you should consult a licensed attorney who is familiar with the laws and procedures of your jurisdiction.

CHELSEA HOUSE PUBLISHERS

VP, New Product Development   Sally Cheney
Director of Production   Kim Shinners
Creative Manager   Takeshi Takahashi
Manufacturing Manager   Diann Grasse

Staff for FREEDOM OF SPEECH

Editor   Patrick M.N. Stone
Production Editor   Jaimie Winkler
Photo Editor   Sarah Bloom
Series and Cover Designer   Keith Trego
Layout   21st Century Publishing and Communications, Inc.

A Haights Cross Communications ⚹ Company

http://www.chelseahouse.com

First Printing

1 3 5 7 9 8 6 4 2

Library of Congress Cataloging-in-Publication Data

Allport, Alan, 1970–
    Freedom of speech / Alan Allport.
      p. cm.—(Point-counterpoint)
Includes index.
    ISBN 0-7910-7370-X
    1. Freedom of speech—United States—Juvenile literature. [1. Freedom of speech.] I. Title. II. Series: Point-counterpoint (Philadelphia, Pa.)
KF4772.Z9 A447 2002
342.73'0853—dc21

                                                            2002015607

||||||||CONTENTS

Introduction
Alan Marzilli, M.A., J.D.
Durham, North Carolina

The debates presented in POINT/COUNTERPOINT are among the most interesting and controversial in contemporary American society, but studying them is more than an academic activity. They affect every citizen; they are the issues that today's leaders debate and tomorrow's will decide. The reader may one day play a central role in resolving them.

Why study both sides of the debate? It's possible that the reader will not yet have formed any opinion at all on the subject of this volume—but this is unlikely. It is more likely that the reader will already hold an opinion, probably a strong one, and very probably one formed without full exposure to the arguments of the other side. It is rare to hear an argument presented in a balanced way, and it is easy to form an opinion on too little information; these books will help to fill in the informational gaps that can never be avoided. More important, though, is the practical function of the series: Skillful argumentation requires a thorough knowledge of *both* sides—though there are seldom only two, and only by knowing what an opponent is likely to assert can one form an articulate response.

Perhaps more important is that listening to the other side sometimes helps one to see an opponent's arguments in a more human way. For example, Sister Helen Prejean, one of the nation's most visible opponents of capital punishment, has been deeply affected by her interactions with the families of murder victims. Seeing the families' grief and pain, she understands much better why people support the death penalty, and she is able to carry out her advocacy with a greater sensitivity to the needs and beliefs of those who do not agree with her. Her relativism, in turn, lends credibility to her work. Dismissing the other side of the argument as totally without merit can be too easy—it is far more useful to understand the nature of the controversy and the reasons *why* the issue defies resolution.

The most controversial issues of all are often those that center on a constitutional right. The Bill of Rights—the first ten amendments to the U.S. Constitution—spells out some of the most fundamental rights that distinguish the governmental system of the United States from those that allow fewer (or other) freedoms. But the sparsely worded document is open to interpretation, and clauses of only a few words are often at the heart of national debates. The Bill of Rights was meant to protect individual liberties; but the needs of some individuals clash with those of society as a whole, and when this happens someone has to decide where to draw the line. Thus the Constitution becomes a battleground between the rights of individuals to do as they please and the responsibility of the government to protect its citizens. The First Amendment's guarantee of "freedom of speech," for example, leads to a number of difficult questions. Some forms of expression, such as burning an American flag, lead to public outrage—but nevertheless are said to be protected by the First Amendment. Other types of expression that most people find objectionable, such as sexually explicit material involving children, are not protected because they are considered harmful. The question is not only where to draw the line, but how to do this without infringing on the personal liberties on which the United States was built.

The Bill of Rights raises many other questions about individual rights and the societal "good." Is a prayer before a high school football game an "establishment of religion" prohibited by the First Amendment? Does the Second Amendment's promise of "the right to bear arms" include concealed handguns? Is stopping and frisking someone standing on a corner known to be frequented by drug dealers a form of "unreasonable search and seizure" in violation of the Fourth Amendment? Although the nine-member U.S. Supreme Court has the ultimate authority in interpreting the Constitution, its answers do not always satisfy the public. When a group of nine people—sometimes by a five-to-four vote—makes a decision that affects the lives of hundreds of millions, public outcry can be expected. And the composition of the Court does change over time, so even a landmark decision is not guaranteed to stand forever. The limits of constitutional protection are always in flux.

These issues make headlines, divide courts, and decide elections. They are the questions most worthy of national debate, and this series aims to cover them as thoroughly as possible. Each volume sets out some of the key arguments surrounding a particular issue, even some views that most people consider extreme or radical—but presents a balanced perspective on the issue. Excerpts from the relevant laws and judicial opinions and references to central concepts, source material, and advocacy groups help the reader to explore the issues even further and to read "the letter of the law" just as the legislatures and the courts have established it.

It may seem that some debates—such as those over capital punishment and abortion, debates with a strong moral component—will never be resolved. But American history offers numerous examples of controversies that once seemed insurmountable but now are effectively settled, even if only on the surface. Abolitionists met with widespread resistance to their efforts to end slavery, and the controversy over that issue threatened to cleave the nation in two; but today public debate over the merits of slavery would be unthinkable, though racial inequalities still plague the nation. Similarly unthinkable at one time was suffrage for women and minorities, but this is now a matter of course. Distributing information about contraception once was a crime. Societies change, and attitudes change, and new questions of social justice are raised constantly while the old ones fade into irrelevancy.

Whatever the root of the controversy, the books in POINT/ COUNTERPOINT seek to explain to the reader the origins of the debate, the current state of the law, and the arguments on both sides. The goal of the series is to inform the reader about the issues facing not only American politicians, but all of the nation's citizens, and to encourage the reader to become more actively involved in resolving these debates, as a voter, a concerned citizen, a journalist, an activist, or an elected official. Democracy is based on education, and every voice counts—so every opinion must be an informed one.

In this volume, Alan Allport examines one of America's fundamental freedoms. The First Amendment declares that "Congress shall make no law . . . abridging the freedom of speech, or of the press. . . . " Although private citizens and the press seem to be entitled to unfettered freedom of expression under the Constitution, the issue is by no means so simple.

The freedoms of speech and of the press are often questioned when others may be harmed by the speech act in question—Should the Ku Klux Klan be allowed to burn crosses in order to intimidate minority groups? Should people be allowed to post pornography on the Internet, where children may have access to it? Should the press be allowed to invade personal privacy or to reveal military secrets? But many argue that that unpopularity of a speech act is precisely why it must be defended. The author examines some of the primary arguments for and against limits on freedom of expression.

Free Speech and the First Amendment

One weekend in February of 2000, Nick Emmett, a college-bound senior at a high school near Seattle in Washington State, decided to create a light-hearted "unofficial" website for the school on his home computer. Prompted by an assignment in a recent writing class, he invented and posted a mock obituary to one of his school-friends. The idea caught on, and as other students heard about the site they asked Nick to write their mock obituaries also. The number of visitors to the site kept increasing, and so Nick added a way for students to vote for the next "death notice." For the first couple of days, everyone praised Nick's site—even some of his teachers, who were impressed by his creativity and could see that it was meant in good fun.

Then a local TV news station did a report about the website that put a very sinister spin on the obituaries, implying that

The tragic events at Columbine High School in April of 1999, when two students (shown here in a security camera image) killed 13 people, caused school authorities across America to tighten up regulations on potentially dangerous student conduct and expression. One high school senior inadvertently caught up in this crackdown, Nick Emmett, successfully challenged his school on First Amendment grounds.

Nick was creating some kind of "hit list." Less than a year had passed since the terrible events at Columbine High School in Colorado, where 13 people were murdered in a shooting rampage, and fears about student violence were still very fresh in local communities throughout America. Nick, who was horrified at the misrepresentation of his website on the TV show, decided to remove it from the Internet immediately.

Two days later, however, he was given a week's suspension by the school authorities. Nick and his parents believed that this punishment was unfair, and so they decided to take the matter to federal court. The judge in the case quickly decided that Nick's First Amendment right to freedom of speech had been violated, and told the school to end the suspension immediately. In the final settlement the school district removed the punishment from Nick's permanent record and agreed to pay his legal fees. Afterwards, Nick said that he was sorry his website had caused so much trouble, but nonetheless believed that "it was good to prove students' rights to free speech."[1]

The growth of the Internet is just one of the reasons why free speech issues at the local community level are becoming ever more complex. High school students have been gossiping about their friends and teachers for as long as anyone can remember, but now that students can build and use sophisticated chat sites on the World Wide Web from their own homes—making this gossip publishable and accessible literally across the globe—should school authorities have the power to control it? Not all of the uses of the Internet are as innocuous as Nick Emmett's. Some student free speech cases have centered on highly offensive personal attacks on classmates and teachers, attacks that have clearly upset and frightened people. The theory of student free speech can mean, in practice, malicious rumors and hurt feelings. And there is a safety issue as well: it is quite true that the Columbine killers discussed their plans on a website prior to the shootings. Free speech law does not protect specific threats, as some students have discovered recently when their comments on the Internet brought expulsion from school. So what is the right balance between fair expression and the rights of the community? What can and cannot be said?

How will the Internet affect the right to free speech?

How has it affected the idea of speech already?

The First Amendment

At the center of all of these issues is the First Amendment to the Constitution of the United States, one of the original ten amendments known collectively as the Bill of Rights that were passed into law in 1791. The First Amendment consists of a single sentence:

> Congress shall make no law respecting an establishment of religion, or prohibiting the free exercise thereof; or abridging the freedom of speech, or of the press; or the right of the people peaceably to assemble, and to petition the government for a redress of grievances.

Probably no other sentence in American history has aroused such passions and opened up so many possibilities as the First Amendment. It is also one of the hardest-working clauses in the whole Constitution, because it entrenches no less than five key rights in a row: freedom from government involvement in religion (sometimes known as the "separation of church and state"); freedom of worship; freedom of speech; freedom of the press—the right to publish without government censorship; and the freedom to assemble to discuss and protest about the issues of the day. The first two rights concerning religion are very much in the news, for example with the recent federal court decision that the "under God" portion of the Pledge of Allegiance is unconstitutional; but while these are both undoubtedly First Amendment rights, they are somewhat different from other issues concerning free speech—and will be addressed in a later book in this series—so they will not be focused on here.

What the free speech protections of the First Amendment say, in essence, is that the U.S. government cannot pass laws that interfere with the rights of American citizens to express their opinions about public or private matters. Originally this applied only to the federal authorities, but later the state and local governments were included, and the Amendment also covers public institutions like schools and colleges. The First Amendment does not mean that Americans are free to say absolutely anything they like whenever and wherever they like: government is allowed some discretionary powers in the public interest. But it does mean that Americans enjoy an unusually large amount of freedom when it comes to speaking their minds. The United States is not unique in having constitutionally protected free speech, but the principle is interpreted more broadly here than in most other countries, even other modern democratic nations. For example, although there is a long tradition of respecting free speech in the United Kingdom, the British do not have an absolute right to it in law. Similarly, there are restrictions on certain types of free expression in

THE LETTER OF THE LAW

From the Sedition Act (Approved July 14, 1798)

[Be it enacted that] if any person shall write, print, utter, or publish, or shall cause or procure to be written, printed, uttered, or published, or shall knowingly and willingly assist or aid in writing, printing, uttering, or publishing any false, scandalous and malicious writing or writings against the government of the United States, or either House of the Congress of the United States, or the President of the United States, with intent to defame the said government, or either House of the said Congress, or the said President, or to bring them, or either of them, into contempt or disrepute, or to excite against them, or either or any of them, the hatred of the good people of the United States, or to excite any unlawful combinations therein, for opposing or resisting any law of the United States, or any act of the President of the United States, done in pursuance of any such law, or of the powers in him vested by the constitution of the United States, or to resist, oppose, or defeat any such law or act, or to aid, encourage or abet any hostile designs of any foreign nation against the United States, their people or government, then such person, being thereof convicted before any court of the United States having jurisdiction thereof, shall be punished by a fine not exceeding two thousand dollars, and by imprisonment not exceeding two years.

France and Germany that would be ruled unconstitutional in the United States.

Since the First Amendment is a constitutional protection, it carries the ultimate authority of the Supreme Court. If Americans feel that their civic rights to free speech have been infringed on by the authorities, they can petition the judiciary to overturn the decision. In most cases a lower federal court reviews the case, although either side, if unsuccessful, can try to appeal the decision to a higher court. If the circumstances are not clear-cut and a definitive interpretation of the law is required, it's possible that the Supreme Court itself will agree to hear the case. The Supreme Court's decision is regarded as the final word on the subject, and the precedent it sets may have an important influence on First Amendment rights for years or even generations to come. Only a later Supreme Court decision can overturn this interpretation in the eyes of the law.

Although it was not part of the original document and was only added a few years later, the First Amendment has been described as the keystone of the whole Constitution. This is because it is only through free expression that the other rights enshrined in that document can be properly protected; tyranny can arise only if the people are powerless to speak out against it. The Founding Fathers believed that the free exchange of opinions was the best guarantee of a healthy and vigorous democracy.

Defining "Speech"

However the Founders themselves personally defined speech, the range of modern free speech protection has extended far beyond the mere spoken word. Speech is now considered to include a whole range of language, gestures, and behaviors; any instance of such expression, linguistic or not, is referred to as a "speech act." One of the more controversial examples of recent years is the

When the Framers protected "speech," what did they mean to protect?

Has the nature of speech changed since then?

deliberate burning of the U.S. flag: although this is obviously not a spoken action, the courts have nonetheless decided that it counts as speech for the purposes of the First Amendment and it is consequently protected. The key factor is that it is an action that *communicates an idea*. The purpose of the First Amendment was to bolster communication within society, and so if an act is judged to be some kind of medium of information or opinion, it is defined as speech. In recent years the Supreme Court has taken an increasingly broad view of this, designating all kinds of behavior as legitimate forms of communication. Although the main focus of the First Amendment has traditionally been on political information and opinion, protected speech does not necessarily have to be overtly political: even commercial information, like advertising, has some protection under the First Amendment, though to a lessor extent than other forms of speech.

One type of speech that is specifically mentioned in the Constitution is the freedom of the press. The Founding Fathers believed that books and newspapers had an important role to play in the maintenance of a civic democracy, as well as unique responsibilities. Today television, film, radio, and the Internet have joined the traditional forms of the press to create a "mass media society," whose great powers and duties will be explored in more detail later in the book.

Unpopular Speech

The First Amendment was not designed to protect someone's right to say that the sky is blue, because that kind of speech doesn't need protection. By definition, opinions that are uncontroversial are not going to be suppressed by the government, or indeed anyone else, for why would they want to suppress them? The heart of free speech protection is to defend *unpopular* ideas or information, speech that other people may want forbidden or kept silent. The most important tests of the First

Amendment arise at its wilder margins, when it is protecting speech that is very controversial or that challenges standard preconceptions and beliefs.

This is not to suggest that unpopular speech is necessarily worthy. Many ideas are unpopular because they are unpleasant, or misleading, or bizarre, or simply insane. Very few Americans would nowadays agree with the kind of "hate speech" propagated by racist fringe groups, for example: the vast majority would prefer to see these ideas disappear for good. But is the best way to tackle hate speech to tolerate it or to ban it? This remains a hotly debated topic, which has become even more urgent with the mass publication possibilities of the Internet. The traditional answer given by supporters of the First Amendment is that it isn't the government's place to decide which beliefs are "good" and which are "evil." Instead, the "marketplace of ideas" should be the proper forum for this type of decision. Just as in the commercial marketplace valuable goods and services rise in demand while shoddy ones are passed by, so in the abstract world of argument worthy ideas will become accepted and bad ones ignored. This sometimes means tolerating opinions that are obnoxious or hateful, but free speech advocates trust in the

FROM THE BENCH

From *Cohen v. California*, 403 U.S. 15 (1971)

To many, the immediate consequence of [the freedom of speech] may often appear to be only verbal tumult, discord, and even offensive utterance. These are, however, within established limits, in truth necessary side effects of the broader enduring values which the process of open debate permits us to achieve. That the air may at times seem filled with verbal cacophony is, in this sense, not a sign of weakness but of strength.

common sense of the people to choose only virtuous ideas in the long term. While the marketplace of ideas, as Thomas Jefferson once wrote to James Madison, is "alloyed with some inconveniences," its good "vastly outweighs the evil."[2] This, at least, is the theory—but it's still the subject of great debate.

While unpopular opinions are often rightly unpopular, it is important to keep in mind that some ideas that are now commonplace were once considered bizarre or dangerous. Anti-slavery campaigners in the early to mid-1800s, for example, were often harassed for their "extreme" views on emancipation and the rights of all people, black and white. Pioneering Victorian feminists who advocated votes for women were depicted as hysterical zealots. Trade unionists faced imprisonment for supporting labor rights. Perhaps current ideas of what are and what are not "normal" beliefs will be considered absurd in years to come.

Which ideas that are difficult to accept today seem likely to become common in the future?

It's not always easy to tell which ideas will be accepted into the mainstream and which will be ultimately forgotten or rejected, and this is another reason why free speech supporters believe as much opinion as possible should be protected by the First Amendment.

Limitations on Speech

There is no absolute right in America to say anything at all, at any time, about anything. Even the most diehard advocates of free speech accept that it must have some practical restrictions in the interests of public safety and in order to protect other kinds of rights. There is no right, for instance, to march into someone else's house uninvited to begin a political oration: the law says that the householder's right to privacy comes first in this case. Nor can someone publish confidential information about troop movements in a newspaper during wartime: national security has to be respected and guaranteed, too. As Supreme Court justice Oliver Wendell Holmes famously put it, "The most stringent protection of free speech would not protect a man in falsely shouting "fire" in a theater."[3] The restrictions that the government can put on speech are, however, carefully defined and subject to constant review to prevent abuse.

Free speech issues are usually divided into two categories: *content* and *time, place, and manner.* The first is concerned with *what* you can say and the second with *when, where, and how* you can say it. Restrictions on speech content are very limited. The traditional restriction in the first half of the 20th century—again, the inspiration of Oliver Wendell Holmes—came as the result of a 1919 Supreme Court case called *Schenck v. United States*, in which an agitator against American involvement in World War I was prosecuted for distributing materials opposing conscription. Although the Justices found against Schenck, the precedent was established that the government could ban speech only if there was a "clear and present danger"[4] of its producing harm to the public. Later, this was clarified and refined in what is called "the *Brandenburg* standard" after the legal case in which it was first used, *Brandenburg v. Ohio* (1969). Brandenburg was a Ku Klux Klan leader who was prosecuted under a state ordinance outlawing speech that advocated lawless behavior. The Supreme Court threw out this conviction, and as a result of its decision speech can now only be suppressed on the grounds of public safety if it is intended, and likely, to produce "imminent lawless action."[5] In other words, vague threats (such as a general speech by a person like Brandenburg or a group that advocates revolution, like the Communist Party) are not enough; the government can only take action in cases where

> **Which is more limiting— content restrictions or time, place, and manner restrictions?**

there is an immediate, demonstrable risk of violence or illegality. There are other content restrictions on the grounds of obscenity and criminal libel, too.

Time, place, and manner restrictions are easier to enforce because they do not totally prevent the communication of ideas: they only limit them in certain contexts. So, for example, city authorities are allowed to require permits in advance for political rallies, on the grounds that they have a responsibility to maintain public order, the smooth flow of traffic, noise control, etc. However, there are conditions to this that the authorities have to abide by: the city government cannot hand out its permits in a partisan way, for instance, allowing some groups to protest and forbidding others from doing the same. Whenever the state interferes in free speech it must do so with an even hand, not favoring any one side in an argument.

Also, the courts generally frown on suppressing speech *before* it is expressed, rather than afterwards: such a restriction is called "prior restraint." Like many American legal principles, the importance—or rather infamy—of prior restraint comes to us through the heritage of British common law.

In what situations is prior restraint acceptable?

In general? In specific cases?

How strong does suspicion have to be?

In 1694 the English Parliament refused to renew an old licensing system for books and periodicals originally created by Henry VIII, arguing that it was a form of unjust political censorship. The United States inherited this belief that licensing and other types of prior restraint were contrary to the spirit of the Bill of Rights because they involved a severe limitation on free expression. Writers, went the argument, should be judged based on what they have written, not on what they might write in the future. Although this sense that prior restraint was unconstitutional lingered throughout early American history, it wasn't until 1931 that the Supreme Court, in its *Near v. Minnesota* decision, formally confirmed that laws practicing prior restraint should usually be struck down.[6]

As these examples show, the First Amendment often clashes with other important privileges and responsibilities, and in specific cases it is the job of the courts to decide which one has the highest priority in the best interests of society. Because free speech is such an important right, its restriction is never considered lightly, however, and the government is permitted to act against it only in genuinely compelling circumstances. Free speech is a constantly negotiated right, one that has its costs as well as its benefits. The following chapters explain some of the principal controversies that have arisen through this negotiation.

Some Ideas Are Dangerous Enough to Merit Restriction

In October of 1976, the Director of Parks and Recreation for the small Chicago suburb of Skokie received a request from a group calling itself the National Socialist Party of America to stage a rally on public ground. The organization, which advocated ugly racial and ethnic policies based on those of Adolf Hitler's Nazi Germany, had not chosen Skokie at random. The township had a large Jewish population, and some of its residents were survivors of the Nazi concentration camps of World War II. The intention of the marchers was clearly provocative, especially as they planned to wear Nazi-style uniforms and carry swastikas and other symbols of the Third Reich. The Skokie Parks District's board of governors refused the request, and in addition filed an

What is the difference between a hate crime and hate speech?

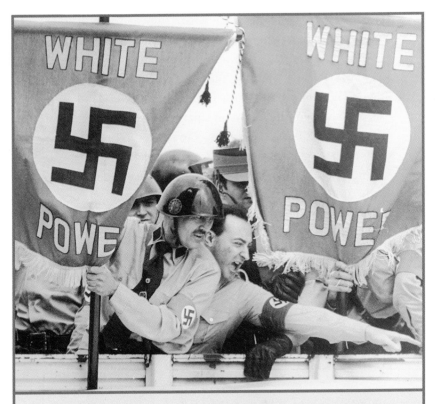

In 1977, the National Socialist Party of America, a racist group, caused great controversy when its right to march through a predominantly Jewish neighborhood of Chicago was successfully defended by the American Civil Liberties Union (ACLU) in the Supreme Court. Here the group's leader, Frank Collin, shouts back at protestors lining a parade route.

injunction in Illinois' Cook County district court to prevent the Nazis from marching in their town. This was the beginning of the *Skokie* controversy—one of the most divisive and emotional cases in First Amendment history, and also an important benchmark in the controversy over the right to express "hate speech."

The *Skokie* affair was a complicated, long-running story involving many lawsuits and counter-suits in both state and federal courts, but in essence what happened was this: The Nazi group asked the Illinois courts to stay, or put on hold, the injunction against them until they could mount a full appeal. This was refused. Having failed at the state level, the Nazis then took their request to the U.S. Supreme Court, and, to the surprise of many, they won: in a narrow five-to-four decision, the Supreme Court forced Illinois to stay its injunction pending appeal.[1] Around the same time, the Skokie town council drew up a set of ordinances banning the wearing of military-style uniforms in political demonstrations, and prohibiting the distribution of material that incited hatred against certain racial or religious groups. The Nazis went to court to overturn these ordinances on First Amendment grounds, and in February of 1978 the federal district court in Illinois ruled that they were indeed unconstitutional. Skokie's case effectively collapsed that October when the Supreme Court refused to hear the township's appeal.[2] In fact, no Nazi ever did march in Skokie—the group ultimately cancelled its rally, claiming that its "moral victory" was success enough—but the Supreme Court's 1978 decision had repercussions far beyond the Chicago suburbs.

Hate speech is also hate crime.

A report by the Federal Bureau of Investigation in 2000 detailed over 8,000 cases of "hate crimes"—offenses against people or property which were motivated by a hatred of another's race, religion, sexual orientation, national origin, or disability.[3] There is a growing debate within the United States about hate crime legislation, and whether criminal behavior involving hate should receive extra punishment in the courts. Hate crimes and hate speech must not be confused, however, for there is an important distinction in law: hate crimes are acts—such as robbery, assault, or murder—which would be clearly illegal and punishable *no matter what their motivation was*. There is no question of hate crimes being protected by the Constitution: nobody in America has a right to harm another person, no matter what the motivation. Nor is active discrimination or harassment in the workplace based on race, sex, religion, etc. allowed. But hate speech—the dissemination of hateful ideas and opinions, without acting on them—is trickier. The expression of political viewpoints lies at the heart of the First Amendment, and there is a much less clear-cut justification for prohibiting or punishing such speech. Cases like the 1978 *Skokie* decision have established the precedent that—so long as it remains speech and not action—hate in America is, effectively, legal and protected.

> **Where is the line between a strongly held opinion and "hate"?**

But why? Traditionally, defenders of free expression have fallen back on an appeal to the marketplace of ideas—or, as Evelyn Beatrice Hall once paraphrased Voltaire, "I disapprove of what you say, but I will defend to the death your right to say it."[4] And after all, speech is not action—so the old claim goes. Yet this division between thought and deed, while it makes for a nice philosophical distinction, is not so easy to see in practice. Words wound emotionally if not physically, and more importantly they can create a culture of resentment and anger which encourages and legitimizes hate crimes: acts of hate are usually pre-empted and accompanied by hate speech, and for society to pretend otherwise—to ignore the causes behind ideologically motivated violence, to argue that speech and action can be neatly decoupled—is self-destructive. The Framers of the Constitution protected speech because they believed the act of communication valuable to society in its own right. What possible worth would have resulted from a Nazi march through Skokie, terrorizing the township's inhabitants and perhaps inciting people to dabble in pro-fascist ideas? The current First Amendment protection of hate speech, however well-meant in principle, hurts precisely those members of society least able to protect themselves—and, moreover, is damaging to the principles of freedom and justice embodied in the U.S. Constitution.

The First Amendment doesn't forbid the control of hate speech.

Despite the Supreme Court's current protection of hate speech, there have been alternative interpretations of the First Amendment that have not been so indulgent. In 1942 the Court sustained the conviction of Walter Chaplinsky, a New Hampshire man who had caused a public disturbance in Rochester and spoken offensively to public officials. In his summary, Justice Frank Murphy spoke of a distinction between "worthwhile" and "worthless" speech. Worthwhile speech contained some social merit; worthless speech was merely obscene, slanderous, or needlessly provocative, and therefore not fit for constitutional protection. Justice Murphy went further and created a category of worthless speech called "fighting words," defined as speech that either "incited an immediate breach of the peace" or—crucially—merely "inflicted injury" on the sensibilities of others. Although it didn't mention the term "hate speech," which hadn't yet been

FROM THE BENCH

From *Chaplinsky v. New Hampshire*, 315 U.S. 568 (1942)

It is well understood that the right of free speech is not absolute at all times and under all circumstances. There are certain well-defined and narrowly limited classes of speech, the prevention and punishment of which has never been thought to raise any Constitutional problem. The English language has a number of words and expressions which by general consent are "fighting words" when said without a disarming smile. . . . [S]uch words, as ordinary men know, are likely to cause a fight.

coined, *Chaplinsky v. New Hampshire* effectively ruled that such expression was not covered under the protections of the First Amendment.[5]

Later Supreme Court rulings overturned much of the *Chaplinsky* decision, including its worthwhile/worthless categories and its broad interpretation of fighting words. Nowadays the "inflicted injury" clause has been dropped, and in order to meet the Court's definition fighting words must be spoken in a face-to-face confrontation where there is a likelihood of an immediate breach of the peace. In fairness, Justice Murphy's ruling was considered vague by many even at the time and probably needed refining by subsequent decisions. But for all its failings it did point the way to another possible evolution of the First Amendment, one that protected genuine public discussion while excluding hateful or deliberately offensive speech. An absolutist stance on free expression is not an inherently more "authentic" reading of the First Amendment, one that automatically adheres to the intentions of the Founding Fathers; all the articles of the Bill of Rights are open to honest differences of interpretation. There is no necessary contradiction between respecting free expression and wishing to restrict hate speech.

The desecration of important symbols should not be protected.

Two of the most emotive examples of a deliberately provocative speech act in recent American history have been the intentional burning or desecration of the Stars and Stripes as a form of public protest, and the burning of crosses in a style made notorious by the "white supremacist" extremists of the Ku Klux Klan. Although the kinds of people conducting these acts are motivated by totally different ideas, the issues involved in flag and cross burning are really the same: must actions that are intended to anger, offend, and in many cases intimidate be protected under the First Amendment simply because they are forms of "political speech"? There is a strong case against this.

The flag of the United States is the most revered symbol of the nation, one that the vast majority of its citizens hold very dear. Historically, the judiciary has not always been hostile to laws banning its deliberate damage: in a 1907 Supreme Court decision Justice John Marshall Harlan wrote that "insults to a flag have been the cause of war, and indignities put upon it, in the presence of those who revere it, have often been resented and sometimes punished on the spot."[6] However, in 1989 and 1990 the Court specifically ruled that burning the flag is a form of constitutionally protected speech. Defenders of this decision have argued that it is important to respect the rights of peaceful demonstrators even if they are behaving in a way that any given observer may find personally objectionable. If the United States begins legislating what kinds of protest are "tasteful" and what kinds are not, it will open the possibility of further restrictions on more important matters—the "slippery slope" argument. But is the slope particularly slippery in the case of flag burning? Does the act of desecrating a flag really communicate any serious political idea or viewpoint that couldn't be better expressed in a more acceptable manner? Is it really plausible that First Amendment rights will be placed in

Is flag burning a form of hate speech?

FROM THE BENCH

From *Texas v. Johnson*, 491 U.S. 397 (1989) (Rehnquist, J., dissenting)

The ideas of liberty and equality have been an irresistible force in motivating leaders like Patrick Henry, Susan B. Anthony, and Abraham Lincoln . . . if those ideas are worth fighting for it cannot be true that the flag that uniquely symbolizes their power is not itself worthy of protection from unnecessary desecration.

jeopardy if flag burning—an act that many citizens would consider repugnant and even hateful—is no longer tolerated by the community?

If anything, cross burning is an even more divisive issue than flag desecration because in its case the intention is not merely to provoke or offend but to terrify. People across the southern United States are only too vividly aware of the symbolic menace of a burning white cross, which has been traditionally used by racist groups as a means of frightening people of different ethnicities and religions, particularly African-Americans. Throughout the 1990s the Supreme Court issued a number of contradictory decisions about cross burning, and the court promised to deliver a clear line on the issue in the fall of 2002.[7] The case for excluding cross burning from the First Amendment is very strong. As an editorial in *The Houston Chronicle* put it: "When a cross is burned in front of a black family's home, the threat is unmistakable . . . groups employ cross-burning as a form of domestic terrorism."[8] The Constitution does not have to be blind to the fact that this kind of speech is really about provoking fear rather than expressing an opinion.

Hate speech can create a "culture of hatred."

Advocates of an absolute right to free speech argue that hate remains relatively harmless so long as it is not translated into action. This, however, ignores the insidious effects of such speech on society as a whole. When ideologically motivated anger is allowed free expression without hindrance from the law, what has been termed a "culture of hatred" can begin to permeate relationships among groups of people and, over time, begin to legitimize acts of violence—even including mass murder. Cultures of this kind have developed in recent years in places as far apart as Europe and Africa. In the former Yugoslavia, accusations against different ethnic groups encouraged the outbreak of a civil war that saw the death of

The burning of crosses, long a symbol of "white supremacist" groups like the Ku Klux Klan, is currently considered a form of protected speech under the First Amendment. Many campaigners against racism argue that cross burning is not a genuine speech act but rather an act of intimidation—and should therefore be punishable by law. In this picture, Klansmen, led by former Grand Wizard David Duke, salute a burning cross.

thousands of Serbs, Croats, and Bosnians. In Rwanda, radio stations openly encouraged people to kill their neighbors, and the result was a genocide involving up to one million victims. This is not to suggest, of course, that the United States faces the prospect of such a catastrophe. But there is a lot of evidence that hate speech, by dehumanizing its targets, can slowly remove social taboos against acts of violence and anger.

Is there value in hate speech?

—————●———————●———————●———————

The defense of hate speech is ultimately a romantic attachment to a certain puritanical theory of society. It assumes that all public discussion has some kind of merit, that words have only rhetorical effect, and that deep down all people are open to rational argument. While one cannot doubt the sincerity behind these assumptions, they are sadly unconnected to the realities of modern American life. It is an unfortunate truth that a small but noisy and dangerous number of citizens are willing to abuse and exploit the freedoms granted to them by the Bill of Rights: they wish to offend, anger, and scare other people whom they dislike simply because of their racial or religious backgrounds, for example, or their sexual orientation. Hate speech is valueless and cannot be countered by force of logic, for it is beyond the reach of reason. If its practitioners choose to nurse their grievances in private, then the state should permit them to do so. But they have no inherent right to express bigotry *in public*. The ideas a country is willing to condone in the open forum say a lot about the kind of society it is, and how well it protects its most vulnerable members. By prohibiting hate speech the United States would be extending, not limiting, its constitutional freedoms.

Banning Dangerous Speech Won't Solve the Problem

In January of 1998 the French film actress Brigitte Bardot was fined the equivalent of about $3,300 for remarks she had made to an extreme right-wing magazine about the Islamic practice of ritual animal slaughter. This was not the first time that the 1960s movie star had courted controversy by her strong opinions about animal rights, opinions which often spill over into derogatory and highly offensive comments about France's large ethnic Arab population; the previous October she had been fined about $1,600 for claiming that France was being "overrun" by Muslims.[1]

Should Brigitte Bardot have been fined for her remarks?

Are the French and German laws on hate speech useful?

If Bardot had been American, it is unlikely that any court would have been able to prosecute her for her unpleasant, but constitutionally protected, remarks. But France, unlike the United States, has ruled that a citizen's right to free speech does not include the right to incite racial, ethnic, or religious hatred, and anti–"hate speech" legislation has been put in place to punish offenders like Bardot. The French are not alone in this: many European countries have hate speech restrictions embedded in their systems of law. In Germany, for example, it is illegal to display symbols associated with the former Nazi government of Adolf Hitler, such as the swastika. Many of the newly emerging democracies of central and eastern Europe either have adopted such laws during the past 10 years or are considering them.

What has been the practical effect of such legislation? On the whole, it has not been very successful. Extreme political groups have not seen any corresponding decline in their popularity. Indeed, in April of 2002 the people of France were rudely awakened to the rising success of the far-right National Front party when its leader, Jean-Marie Le Pen—whose campaigns have included appeals to anti-Americanism and attacks on immigration—won one of the two available places in the run-off for the national presidency. Le Pen was ultimately defeated in his election bid by a comfortable margin, but his support shocked many people. Since Le Pen's near-run challenge, other dramatic events in France have highlighted the deficiencies of hate-speech laws. When in July of 2002 a neo-Nazi supporter attempted to murder the newly re-elected president, Jacques Chirac, the French courts responded by banning the would-be assassin's political party and its associated website. But this had no discernible effect on the group: it simply moved its site to a new location on the Internet, and indeed claimed that because of the controversy its number of monthly hits had more than doubled to 100,000.[2]

What these examples show is that restrictions on speech, however well intentioned and carefully crafted, are not the best way to tackle the underlying problem of political hatred. Not only is there little evidence that they suppress extremist ideas, but on the contrary they can actually fan the flames of hatred by giving

extremists a mystique of martyrdom. The long-term conse-
quences of hate speech laws are usually farcical (as in the "campus
speech code" movement of the 1980s) or sinister (as in countries
such as South Africa during its Apartheid era). To criticize hate
speech restrictions is not to downplay the genuine danger of
extremism at the fringes of modern American society. But the best
way to neutralize these dangers is by using free speech against
them, rather than trying to artificially narrow the range of debate.

A democracy must trust the judgment of its citizens.

Hate speech is one of the toughest challenges to a belief in the
First Amendment right of free expression. Even the American Civil
Liberties Union (ACLU), which has traditionally taken a very
strong line in supporting controversial uses of free speech, has been
divided by the merits of defending
hate. As the ACLU freely admits, the
danger of allowing hateful words to go
unchecked cannot be ignored: it is
arguable that if European society had
taken more notice of the hate-filled
rhetoric emerging from Germany
and Italy during the 1930s then the
horrors of World War II might
have been avoided. The temptation
to restrict some of the ugliest expres-
sions of hatred based on differences of race, religion, ethnicity,
or sexuality sometimes feels overwhelming.

Can citizens be trusted to form their own opinions?

What level of education is necessary for an informed opinion to be possible?

Did the Constitution always trust the judgment of the people?

However, a rush to hasty action—even with the best of objec-
tives—is very dangerous. Hate speech laws turn out to be more
damaging than the speech they oppose because they undermine
confidence in the very principles of democratic debate, and hence
democracy itself. Free speech defenders are not naïve about the
motivations of extremist political groups such as the Nazis who
wanted to march in Skokie: they believe that these groups are not

sincere in their pleas for "tolerance" and that to some extent they are exploiting the First Amendment. But however risky it is to romanticize free speech, it is even riskier to be cynical about it. The premise behind anti–hate speech laws is too often that of the pessimist who does not really trust citizens to make sensible decisions of their own free will. Sadly, there are always going to be a few people in any society for whom that is true. But the historical experience of the United States shows that, on the whole, the public can be trusted so long as the marketplace of ideas is operating to distinguish good ideas from bad. Faith in the rationality and decency of the American people is implicit within the country's constitutional system, and to abandon this would be to chip away belief in the whole democratic apparatus.

Hate speech legislation is a clumsy and dangerous tool.

The theory behind hate speech laws is tenuous, but what about their practical application? Modern examples of this can be found mostly outside the United States, for it has become effectively

FROM THE BENCH

The Right to Be Foolish

U.S. courts have frequently ruled that freedom of speech includes the right to dangerous beliefs. In *Baumgartner v. United States* (1944), the Supreme Court ruled that a naturalized German-American could not be stripped of his citizenship even though he had often made irresponsible remarks praising the Nazi regime. Justice Frankfurter argued that foolish and immoderate speech has a place in a democratic culture:

> One of the prerogatives of American citizenship is the right to criticize public men and measures—and that means not only informed and responsible criticism but the freedom to speak foolishly and without moderation. Our trust in the good sense of the people on deliberate reflection goes deep.

> —*Baumgartner v. United States*, 322 U.S. 665 (1944)

impossible since key Supreme Court rulings like *Cohen v. California* (1971) to construct a hate speech ordinance in the United States that will survive constitutional scrutiny.[3] The results of the French attempt to limit hateful speech were poor. One of the other conclusions one can draw from an international survey is that it has quite often been oppressive governments that have shown the most enthusiasm for hate speech legislation. In the former Soviet Union, such laws were used to punish "defamatory" critics of the Communist Party regime. Turkish scholars investigating human rights abuses against the Kurdish minority have been prosecuted for supposedly spreading ethnic rancor. Perhaps the most extreme example is the Republic of South Africa in its Apartheid era: during this period the government

Do hate speech laws make martyrs of the groups that violate them?

banned all kinds of films and publications attacking its racial policies on the grounds that they incited hatred. Even the well-known TV movie adaptation of Alex Haley's novel *Roots* was prohibited, because "a substantial number of blacks would . . . substantially experience great or greater hate against the white [race] as a result of seeing this film."[4] Clearly, these regimes were interested not in genuinely combating extremist ideas but in increasing their own control of public expression. Anti–hate speech laws gave them a perfect tool to do this. Proponents of restrictions on hate speech complain that the First Amendment is exploited by "hatemongers," forgetting that anti-hate laws can themselves be much more easily abused.

Speech codes are inherently counterproductive.

Perhaps the best example of the shortsightedness of attempts to limit offensive speech is provided by the curious rise and fall of the "campus speech code" campaign across U.S. universities and colleges during the late 1980s and early 1990s.

In 1986 and 1987 the higher education community across America was stunned by a number of racially charged incidents

Novelist Alex Haley achieved great success in the 1970s with his epic biographical novel *Roots*, which told the story of an 18th-century African warrior's capture by European slave traders and of the lives of his descendants in the United States. Ironically, Haley's book was banned in Apartheid-era South Africa; the government claimed it was a form of "hate speech" that would be racially divisive.

involving students. Offensive signs and messages were posted in public places or mailed to individuals, and in one notorious case there was a drunken campus brawl between opposing white and black baseball fans. What made these cases especially troubling is that they frequently involved some of the best universities in the country, such as Stanford, Dartmouth, and Brown. If even these elite institutions were infected by racist ideas, then it seemed as if a plague of intolerance was affecting America's education system. In an attempt to combat this, schools began to create rules of acceptable student conduct that became known collectively as "campus speech codes." The codes differed from school to school, and some were more carefully prepared than others. Stanford's, for example, was quite narrowly drawn up to punish only "fighting words" of the type already ruled unprotected in the Supreme Court's 1942 *Chaplinsky* case. The University of Michigan's, on the other hand, was extremely broad, outlawing "any behavior, verbal or physical, that stigmatizes or victimizes an individual on the basis of race," as well as a host of other perceived wrongdoings.[5]

It wasn't long after the codes were introduced that their flaws started to become apparent. Lecturers complained that the codes had a "chilling effect" on classroom discussion, discouraging students from raising controversial topics for fear that they might run afoul of a disciplinary charge. It seemed absurd that universities, which of all places in society should have encouraged critical inquiry and free debate, were now some of the least free speech forums in America. At the University of Michigan, minority students ironically ended up being charged far more often with code violations than whites. In 1989 a Michigan graduate student challenged the code in federal district court and the judge speedily declared it unconstitutional, condemning its vagueness and declaring that "the University had no idea what the limits of the policy were and was essentially making up the rules as it went along."[6] Other legal defeats followed, and the impetus of the campus speech code movement sagged. In 1995 even Stanford's more limited code was overturned, despite the defense that Stanford was a private institution and hence not bound by First Amendment responsibilities. (This failed because California law explicitly bound private colleges to honor free speech rights.) By the end of the decade campus speech codes were effectively dead, and even though some colleges did not repeal their codes they abandoned any attempt to enforce them.

———————●————————●————————●———————

"The road to Hell is paved with good intentions," according to the proverb. This neatly sums up the hate speech law issue. There is no doubt that offensive, emotionally charged speech will always be a difficult test of the American commitment to free expression. The fear that hate speech can instill in communities is genuine, and it would be glib to simply state that "words cannot hurt" and leave the matter at that. But there is no contradiction between challenging anger while being at the same time opposed to heavy-handed censorship. For one thing, a defense of speech is not necessarily a defense of action: much violent conduct (such as the burning of crosses or posting of offensive symbols on someone else's private property) goes well beyond the constitutional understanding of "speech" and can clearly be prosecuted on the more straightforward grounds of trespassing or criminal damage. For another, the First Amendment is the natural friend of all minorities or oppressed groups because it gives them the tools to take their case to the people. Rather than trying to suppress the superficial symptoms of hate which bubble up through speech, one should be looking for its more profound causes and neutralizing them by positive and proactive measures—education being above all the best antidote to hatred. To genuinely fight hate one should *use* free speech, not limit it.

> **What regulations have a chilling effect on legal activity around you? Why are these regulations in place?**

Obscene Expression Should Not Be Protected

In the fall of 1989, the chamber of the United States Senate was the unusual forum for a debate about the merits—or lack thereof—of some of the most provocative and controversial works of photography in cutting-edge American art. The storm centered in particular on the portfolios of two photographers: Robert Mapplethorpe, whose work involved explicit homoerotic images, and Andreas Serrano, who had exhibited a number of pictures using religious icons in allegedly blasphemous ways. The instigator of the debate was the North Carolina Republican Senator Jesse Helms, a self-described conservative firebrand who throughout his career had taken a strong line on issues concerning traditional

Who should decide which artists and projects are funded by tax money? How?

What if a funded artist produces something other than she said or thought she would?

40

morality and religious values. Despite Helms' revulsion for the work of Mapplethorpe and Serrano, however, they were not the direct targets of his wrath. That role fell to the National Endowment for the Arts (NEA), a federal government agency created in 1965 to provide funding and support for institutional art centers such as museums and galleries, as well as individual artists. Throughout the 1980s conservative watchdogs had become increasingly unhappy with the NEA's choices of supported art projects, believing that many of them were simply obscene or irreverent and skewed towards left-wing political ideas. Helms successfully proposed a new ruling that prevented the NEA from supporting any artwork judged "indecent" or which "denigrated, debased, or defiled" on the basis of race, religion, sex, nationality, etc. Grant recipients were also required to sign an oath promising not to produce obscene material.

The Senate ruling provoked an equally strong counter-reaction from the artistic community, which assailed these new restrictions as censorship and a violation of First Amendment

The NEA Saga — Censorship or Common Sense?

In the late 1980s and early 1990s, the National Endowment for the Arts (NEA) was lambasted by a number of conservative politicians, notably Senator Jesse Helms (R-NC), for its use of public funds to support artwork that many considered obscene. Critics called this an attempt at indirect censorship, but defenders said it was sound judgment. Helms himself argued:

The so-called art community fails to understand — or deliberately refuses to understand — that a difference exists between an artist's right to free expression, and his right to have the Government, that is to say the taxpayers, pay him for his work. . . . I reiterate that there is a fundamental difference between government censorship, the preemption of publication or production, and government's refusal to pay for such publication and production.

—Senate debate, July 26, 1989

rights. Censorship, or the deliberate government prohibition of speech, is a taboo word in the American system; it has always sparked angry resistance from those citizens who see it as inimical to the principles of the Constitution. Both the NEA obscenity clause and the oath were quickly challenged in court and thrown out.[1] In response, the Senate brought in a new provision dropping the oath and merely requiring the NEA to consider "decency" as a factor in making spending decisions. With the size of its overall budget under increasing pressure from Congressional critics, the NEA strove to accommodate the Senate's demands, but in 1992 it found itself taken to court by a group of artists whose applications for funding had been allegedly overturned on the new decency standard. The case was settled in the artists' favor, the judge ruling that the "decency" requirement was too vague to be complied with.[2] It seemed by this that Helms' campaign against the policies of the NEA had been thwarted, but instead the focus of his efforts shifted to simply cutting the NEA's budget, which he accomplished with more success. By the approach of the new millennium, with the NEA a much-weakened institution, it seemed to many in the art world that the legal victories of the early 1990s had been temporary at best.

But did Helms' attack on the NEA really constitute censorship? Supporters of the obscenity and decency standards argued that it was nothing of the sort. After all, the Senate was not actually trying to ban the distribution or display of Mapplethorpe's or Serrano's photographs (though in an unrelated case, a Cincinnati arts center was unsuccessfully prosecuted in 1990 for holding a Mapplethorpe exhibition).[3] All Helms and his lobby were trying to do was to prevent federal money—taxpayers' money, ultimately—from being used to support such work, which a large proportion of the American public probably saw as lewd and without genuine artistic merit. Artists might have a right to create whatever they see fit. But does the state have an equal responsibility to support them financially no matter how shocking their work? To Helms and others, this seemed like an absurd abuse of the constitutional claim to free expression.

Obscenity is a valid category in American law.

The NEA affair underscores the continuing controversy over whether obscene speech ought to be protected under the First Amendment. Historically the Supreme Court's rulings on obscenity have varied depending on the specifics of the case as well as the social and political climate of the times. The vagueness of some of the language does not help either: people commonly speak of "obscenity," "indecency," and "pornography" as though they were the same thing, but in legal terms they are very different. As of 2002, the Court continues to uphold (with a few minor tweaks) a 1973 decision, *Miller v. California,* which says that *obscene* expression is unprotected by the First Amendment but that *indecent* expression—a less provocative form of speech—is protected.[4] So what is obscenity, as opposed to mere indecency? *Miller* defines it through a series of content tests that must be met. The traditional mixing-in of religious heresy—which the Supreme Court now explicitly upholds as protected speech—has in the past made the definition especially complicated.

> To what extent should taxpayers be empowered to decide where their tax money goes?

Even though the precise definition of obscenity may remain a little blurred, there is enough general agreement—as Supreme Court Justice Potter Stewart famous remarked, "I know it when I see it"[5]—to make a category of unprotected speech possible and necessary. Not every form of literature or art that contains sexual content is without value to society, and indeed some challenging works—such as the novels of D.H. Lawrence or James Joyce—are now seen as ground-breaking. But other types of "speech" may well be prurient, offensive, or disgusting and have no genuine redeeming qualities. Not every explicit work is a *Lady Chatterley's Lover* or *Ulysses* awaiting discovery; more likely, it is simply crude. In an age of rapidly changing technology, when it is becoming increasingly difficult for parents to monitor what information their children are receiving from sources like the Internet, it is all the more incumbent on society to protect minors from the worst of human nature.

Controversial publisher Larry Flynt, founder and owner of the pornographic magazine *Hustler*, has been arrested and tried many times on charges of obscenity. While Flynt's opponents dismiss him as a "smut peddler" who courts controversy simply to generate sales, others argue that his magazine's provocative content, not always popular, needs to be defended on important First Amendment grounds.

Obscenity can be an issue of civil rights.

Traditionally, advocates of greater restrictions on obscene speech made their case on the grounds of "community standards"—that is, they argued that if a form of expression was considered highly offensive by the bulk of the population in a certain area, the local authorities should be permitted to restrict it. But this led to complaints about the "tyranny of the majority," since individuals were having to submit to the tastes of their neighbors. During the early 1980s a number of feminist lawyers and writers moved away from community standards and made the more innovative claim that sexually explicit material should be constitutionally unprotected because it violates the *Fourteenth* Amendment's provision that all citizens must receive equal protection of the laws. As was discussed in the opening chapter, the First Amendment exists in parallel with a host of other civil rights, and despite its importance it does not automatically trump the priorities of other constitutional guarantees. Some free speech activists, such as Mary Ellen Gale, the former leader of the Southern California branch of the ACLU, were particularly keen to stress the importance of the Fourteenth Amendment in partnership with the First.

Two influential anti-pornography campaigners—Catherine MacKinnon, a University of Chicago Law Professor, and the writer Andrea Dworkin—have suggested that, because of their demeaning and discriminatory effects on women, many writings and images that do not fall within the current *Miller* definition of obscenity are nonetheless forms of sexual discrimination and thus ought to be unlawful because of the 1964 Civil Rights Act, which was based on the protections of the Fourteenth Amendment. Why, ask MacKinnon and Dworkin, are the rights of women to enjoy safety and freedom from discrimination under this Amendment continually ignored in favor of the commercial speech rights of people who produce pornography? MacKinnon and Dworkin say that porno-graphic materials create an environment of hostility and hatred towards women and that the Supreme Court should be no more tolerant of obscenity than it is of racial or sexual discrimination in the workplace. This legal case has yet to be accepted by the courts. It is, however, an important assertion of what has been called "the missing language of responsibility" in constitutional issues. Instead of the onus constantly being on the defense of individual rights, however foolishly or dangerously they are used, shouldn't the state equally defend the wider community and the need of society as a whole to be free from offensive and demeaning imagery?

> **Does pornography violate civil rights? If so, then whose?**
>
> **Does it create hostility, or simply express it, or neither?**
>
> **How might it create hostility?**

The Internet has made obscenity a bigger problem than ever.

Ever since the explosion in Internet use in the early 1990s, the legal system has been trying to catch up with this new, enor-mously powerful but unpredictable medium of communication. One of the most pressing problems has been the supervision of children in cyberspace: the Internet provides unprecedented opportunities for young people to access information and ideas, but it also exposes them to new dangers. Not only is there a wealth of material inappropriate for the young available on the World Wide Web, but the anonymity afforded by the

Internet has in some cases allowed "cyber-stalkers" in chatrooms to target, harass, and even instigate abuse of minors.

The government's attempts to regulate this ever-expanding territory in the interests of protecting children have not been very successful so far. The most famous example of this was the 1996 Communications Decency Act (CDA), which forbade Internet users from displaying sexually explicit content online unless they had provided some kind of electronic filtering system that restricted access. This act was vigorously opposed by a lobby including the ACLU, the American Library Association (ALA), and a number of professional media organizations. These groups argued that filtering was better handled at the user's end by commercial software that blocked certain websites and newsgroups. But these user filters are not always effective, and parents—who often know a good deal less about the family computer than their children—are too often technically unable to use them properly. The idea that there is a compelling issue of free expression at stake in allowing access to pornographic material is not very convincing. As Kristi Hamick of the Family Research Council said, "To pretend that our nation would somehow end if there weren't hard-core pornography within a child's reach is not only disingenuous, it's uncivilized."[6]

Should minors be allowed access to content that currently is considered inappropriate for them?

Which content, and why? Why is it currently restricted?

In recent years the focus has shifted to the role of public libraries. The 2000 Children's Internet Protection Act (CIPA) requires that any library receiving federal funding must use an appropriate kind of blocking software to prevent minors from accessing obscene or pornographic online content. A lobby similar to that which opposed the CDA in 1996 has challenged CIPA, and in mid-2002 the issue still awaited a final decision by the Supreme Court. Although most libraries and librarians have criticized the requirements of the Act, some have not—a fact that the U.S. Justice Department, which is defending the case, has been quick to point out. For example, the Fulton County Public Library in Rochester, Indiana has been using blocking software to ban sexually explicit material from its workstations, and according to its director, David Ewick, the experience has been very positive and has created no conflict with the library's mission to provide information to the general public.[7] As this example shows, it is not very convincing to say that a library's function will be compromised if it shields children from content that is generally considered inappropriate.

> **How far does a public library's responsibility to provide information extend?**
>
> **Should there be methods of restricting access to some material?**

------●------------●------------●------

Restrictions against obscenity in the United States have not always been fair. But a concept can have been exploited or distorted historically without losing its inherent value. It is an unfortunate truth that there is a great deal of "expression" in 21st-century America that is without any genuine usefulness to society. It may be big business—as the vast profits of the new Internet "porn kings" demonstrate—but that does not make it acceptable. Whether obscenity is wrong because it offends local community standards, acts as a form of harassment against women, or threatens children, the government should have the power to regulate it appropriately. This doesn't—and in fact, shouldn't—mean that all provocative or controversial art, literature, and speech should be prohibited. It does, however, mean that there should be a distinction maintained between forms of expression that genuinely contribute to society's sum of knowledge, as opposed to material that is simply intended to exploit.

Government Should Not Decide What Is Obscene

In 1995, Missouri computer repair technician David Spohr, who had recently signed up with the America Online (AOL) Internet service, decided to use the web space provided as part of his membership to create a fan site devoted to one of his favorite celebrities, the notorious stand-up comic Lenny Bruce. For five years the site existed peacefully, until in August of 2000 Spohr suddenly received an e-mail from AOL notifying him that portions of his site contained "inappropriate" material and were being summarily deleted from the server. "I was shocked at first," said Spohr, "then somewhat amused and disturbed." After he

> Do the major Internet providers have a right, or a responsibility, to monitor content — or should the Internet be as free a domain as possible?
>
> Does the providers' financial interest in their sites make a difference?

complained to AOL, the company relented from its decision and allowed the offending portions of the website to be returned. As *USA Today* put it in a story about Bruce's latter-day brush with the authorities, "Thirty-four years after his death, the controversial comedian is still being hounded for his satirical stabs at government, religion, and American mores."[1]

It was a story that would have been wryly familiar to Bruce himself, who spent much of his troubled career in the 1950s and 1960s fending off injunctions against his "obscene" comic skits. Bruce's act was not for the faint-hearted: he took brutal aim at such sensitive targets as religion, politics, and sex, and he was not afraid to use language and imagery that many people found uncomfortable. Arrested six times between 1961 and 1964 on obscenity charges, Bruce was found not guilty by appeals courts in every case; but the strain of fending off multiple convictions took its toll on the private life of the comic, and he died of a drug overdose in 1966. By the time of his death, however, Bruce had become a celebrated figure in the campaign to broaden First

Lenny Bruce

The raucous stand-up comedian Lenny Bruce was tried on obscenity charges several times in the 1960s. Despite Bruce's frequent use of foul and irreverent language, some critics considered his work an important form of social commentary. A website on Bruce cites a letter from a New York pastor in 1963; the text typifies a positive interpretation often applied to controversial artists:

> Clearly your intent is not to excite sexual feelings or to demean but to shock us awake to the realities of racial hatred and invested absurdities about sex and birth and death ... to move toward sanity and compassion. It is clear that you are intensely angry at our hypocrisies (yours as well as mine) and at the highly subsidized mealy-mouthism that passes as wisdom.

—*www.freenetpages.co.uk/hp/lennybruce/lanier.txt*

Lenny Bruce's career as a stand-up comedian was interrupted during the early 1960s by charges of obscenity. Bruce believed that the real reason why the authorities were trying to punish him was that his commentary on American politics and society was considered too dangerous. Here Bruce is shown at a London airport in 1963 after the British government temporarily relented on its ban against his entering the U.K.

Amendment rights of free expression in America, and he counted among his supporters such popular celebrities as the TV comedian and host Steve Allen.

In hindsight, what is surprising about the Lenny Bruce controversy is how tame so many of his "obscenities" now seem—the kind of language he was arrested for can now commonly be heard on such mainstream TV channels as HBO, for example. In fact, the closer one looks at Bruce's story, the clearer it becomes that his real crime, in the eyes of many public officials at the time, was not really obscenity but a kind of secular blasphemy—in other words, his disrespect towards the cherished political and social beliefs of the age. Bruce was performing in a period of violent change in the United States, when traditional centers of authority like religion and government were under attack for their supposed hypocrisies and their complicity in injustices like the racial segregation of the southern United States. Bruce was doing something far more dangerous than uttering a few "bad words"—he was in his clownish way making an important point about the deep flaws in contemporary American society. The obscenity charges were just a convenient way of censoring Bruce's more important criticisms of racism, anti-Semitism, and other ugly realities. Ironically, given his reputation in the 1960s as one of the country's most deviant heretics, Bruce considered himself to be a patriot: he believed passionately in the constitutional liberties of the Bill of Rights, and felt that it was his opponents that were dishonoring American principles, not him.

Lenny Bruce's story is highly instructive, because it demonstrates how accusations of obscenity are too often just an indirect way for people in power to silence those who have radical things to say about society. The continuing definition of obscenity as a form of unprotected speech by the Supreme Court is vague, arbitrary, and irrelevant to the genuine problems of, say, keeping women and children safe from harassment or abuse. The law already makes it clear that specific forms of exploitative material that almost nobody accepts as legitimate—for example, pornography involving minors—are totally unprotected by the First Amendment and open to prosecution; such restrictions are entirely proper and would survive the end of obscenity as a legal category. But the current restrictions on certain types of sexually explicit speech are irrelevant to these real concerns.

Why does the United States criminalize sexually explicit material involving children?

The concept of obscenity is obsolete.

Throughout its history the Supreme Court has often redefined its understanding of what obscenity is, but the surprising thing is that it has never really questioned *why* there should be such a category of unprotected speech in the first place. The Court has largely accepted it as an eternal truth, with little or no discussion. The explanation for this is largely historical. The American legal system inherited as part of its British heritage the concept of religious heresy, sometimes called blasphemy or sacrilege, which included prohibitions on "bad" language but which was really focused more on questions of doctrine—the teachings of disfavored Christian sects and the denial of conventional religious practices altogether. During the 20th century, as the United States developed an increasingly secular government system under the First Amendment's separation of church and state, these religious elements were slowly abandoned. In a 1952 Supreme Court decision called *Burstyn v. Wilson*, it was ruled that the New York authorities could not ban an Italian movie called *The Miracle* for being irreverent toward the Catholic Church.[2] In *Epperson v. Arkansas* (1968), the Court also ruled that states could not prohibit the teaching of Darwinian evolution in schools on "sacrilegious" grounds.[3] As the religious core of blasphemy was stripped out, only the rules pertaining to indecent language and sexually explicit display—which were not the focus of heresy law anyway—remained. So in the 21st century the United States is essentially stuck with the surviving remnants of an otherwise obsolete legal concept.

Some dissenting members of the Supreme Court that produced the *Miller v. California* definition of obscenity in 1973 (which survives largely intact today) were arguing this thirty years ago. Justice William Brennan, who had earlier been a supporter of decency laws, wrote that he had changed his mind about obscenity altogether. He now believed that it was virtually impossible to draw up a definition of obscenity that was clear and unambiguous, and thus all obscenity laws "failed to give fair notice" to the citizen—in other words, they were so hazy that a person could not be sure in advance whether she was

FROM THE BENCH

What Is "Obscenity"?

Not all of the Supreme Court justices were persuaded by the logic of the *Miller* ruling on obscenity. Justice Douglas wrote an important dissenting opinion, denying the possibility of a coherent legal definition of obscenity:

> There are no constitutional guidelines for deciding what is and what is not "obscene." The Court is at large because we deal with tastes and standards of literature. What shocks me may be sustenance for my neighbor. What causes one person to boil up in rage over one pamphlet or movie may reflect only his neurosis, not shared by others. We deal here with a regime of censorship which, if adopted, should be done by constitutional amendment after full debate by the people.

Under the *Miller* standard, In order for speech to be declared legally obscene, it must meet all of the following criteria:

> (a) the average person, applying contemporary community standards, would find that the work, taken as a whole, appeals to the prurient interest;
> (b) the work depicts or describes, in a patently offensive way, sexual conduct specifically defined by the applicable state law; and
> (c) the work, taken as a whole, lacks serious literary, artistic, political, or scientific value.

> —*Miller v. California*, 413 U.S. 15 (1973)

committing a crime. Failure to give fair notice like this is considered to be inherently unjust in the Anglo-American philosophy of law. Brennan argued that, instead of the government acting as a morality censor, all adult citizens should be allowed to make private decisions about what was personally acceptable to them—although he still believed that the courts had a responsibility to intervene when children or unwilling persons were involved. Brennan and the other dissenters were outvoted, though, and *Miller v. California* became the standard.[4]

Does an American citizen have a right to say or do obscene things? When, where, and in what forms?

Obscenity law is frequently abused.

One of the most notorious abuses of obscenity law in American history, and an example that still carries lessons for the modern day, is the 19th-century "vice squads" of Anthony Comstock.

Anthony Comstock was a New England dry-goods clerk who moved to New York City in 1867. As an extreme Puritan fundamentalist, he was appalled by the "filth" that he encountered in the big city, and he was determined to act unilaterally to end it. By enlisting the support of some powerful local industrialists Comstock created the New York Society for the Suppression of Vice, which he used to track down and arrest alleged purveyors of vice within the city. In 1873 Comstock successfully lobbied Congress to pass a postal censorship law, known thereafter as the Comstock Act, which prohibited the distribution of "obscene" literature. Comstock's interpretation of obscenity was extremely broad: works included under the Comstock ban included Voltaire's *Candide,* Walt Whitman's *Leaves of Grass,* and Daniel Defoe's *Moll Flanders,* and especially any material that dealt with contraception. Comstock's influence at the height of his powers was such that he was essentially the sole arbiter of what could and could not be written in America, and his extreme religiosity became the benchmark for all definitions of "decency."

He became a law unto himself, and sometimes used his authority to carry out private grudges—he ensured, for example, that the works of the English playwright George Bernard Shaw were prohibited because Shaw had insulted Comstock for his self-righteousness. The Comstock vice squads became a source of political power in the big cities of the Northeast, and they were used not merely to punish pornographers but also to legitimize the surveillance of citizens on political and religious grounds. It is worth noting that the Comstock Act remains part of U.S. law, and was indeed upheld as constitutional by the Supreme Court in 1957.[5]

> Which issues of free speech are really moral issues—and how great is the influence of morality in First Amendment debates?
>
> Should a government enforce morality? Whose?

The Internet should not be censored on grounds of obscenity.

The high-tech world of cyberspace might seem a long way from Anthony Comstock's Victorian dry goods store, but in the early 1990s it seemed that the spirit of Comstock had returned to haunt the Internet. The innovative nature of this new technology meant that an important question had to be answered before its free speech status could be ascertained: should the Internet be treated as a form of print material, or as a form of broadcasting? This was important because First Amendment rights are not necessarily the same from medium to medium. Film and television companies are subject to much greater restrictions than newspaper editors over what they can depict to certain age groups—for example through the Motion Picture Association of America (MPAA) ratings for movies. Although the interactive structure of the Internet is a lot closer to newspaper publication than to the one-way medium of television, computer systems with their large color monitors bear a strong physical resemblance to TV sets—and Internet advocates were worried that judges, who might not be very familiar with the technology of cyberspace, would presume from this vague similarity that graphics-heavy systems like the World Wide Web were indeed a form of television.

The U.S. government's first major attempt to regulate Internet traffic, the 1996 Telecommunications Act, assumed that the broadcasting model would be the standard for the future. Bundled into the Telecommunications Act was the notorious Communications Decency Act (CDA), which made it a criminal offense to disseminate materials that are "indecent" (but not technically obscene under the *Miller v. California* definition) to minors online without making a reasonable attempt to restrict minors' access. There was even a late-added amendment to the CDA that made the sending of abortion information on the Internet punishable by up to 5 years in jail or a fine of up to $250,000—which even the Justice Department admitted from the outset would be unenforceable.[6]

THE LETTER OF THE LAW

From the Communications Decency Act of 1996

(e) Whoever . . .

1. knowingly within the United States or in foreign communications with the United States by means of telecommunications device makes or makes available any indecent comment, request, suggestion, proposal, [or] image to any person under 18 years of age regardless of whether the maker of such communication placed the call or initiated the communication; or

2. knowingly permits any telecommunications facility under such person's control to be used for an activity prohibited by paragraph (1) with the intent that it be used for such activity,

shall be fined not more than $100,000 or imprisoned not more than two years or both.

Four months after it was passed into law, a three-judge federal panel in Philadelphia reviewed the CDA and, in a 215-page report, threw out the new regulations entirely on the grounds that the Internet was clearly a medium closer to print than to broadcasting. "[T]he CDA would necessarily reduce the speech available to adults. . . . [T]his is a constitutionally intolerable result," wrote one of the judges.[7] The Philadelphia decision was confirmed by the Supreme Court the following year: the Internet was officially shown to be a medium with the same rights to First Amendment protection as books and newspapers. The anti-censorship lobby had won—for the time being, at least.

———•———•———•———

In the United States today, "indecency" is a protected form of speech and "obscenity" is not. But the Justices of the Supreme Court have little clearer idea of the precise distinction between these two categories than any other group of American citizens. According to the 1973 *Miller* standard, obscene speech "lacks serious literary, artistic, political, or scientific value"—the "SLAPS" test— but this is such a subjective judgment that it fails to give fair notice. It would, in fact, be vastly preferable for the United States to abandon the old religious-moral baggage of obscenity once and for all, and to accept the principle that consenting adults should be trusted to make their own decisions about what they read or view. This would in no way interfere with society's need to prevent genuinely dangerous imagery, such as that involving children for example. But it would finally bring a close to the grim Comstock era and the exploitations of the law that were used against "heretics" like Lenny Bruce.

Do the words *obscenity* and *indecency* deserve a place in the modern world? If so, then what is it?

The "Freedom of the Press" Should Be Restricted

In 1963, a group of relatively unskilled kidnappers led by a California businessman, Barry Keenan, abducted the 19-year-old son of legendary singer Frank Sinatra from a hotel in Lake Tahoe and held him at gunpoint for several days until he was released unharmed. The criminals were speedily caught and Keenan served a four-year prison sentence for his part in the bizarre affair. Thirty-five years later, Keenan, long freed from jail, was paid $450,000 by a Hollywood production company for the movie rights to his story. When Frank Sinatra Jr. heard about the latter-day windfall of his former kidnapper he was angered at the thought that his frightening ordeal had made the felon wealthy, and he decided to have the payment challenged in California state court.[1]

He was able to do this because California, like many U.S. states, had passed a "Son of Sam" law in the early 1990s that required convicted criminals to hand over any profits they received from the retelling of their stories in book, TV, or film form as compensation to the original victims. "Son of Sam" was a reference to the nickname of the notorious 1970s New York City serial killer David Berkowitz: the first Son of Sam law had been passed in New York after Berkowitz's conviction, because book publishers were allegedly offering a fortune for the rights to his autobiography (although Berkowitz never took advantage of any of these offers, and so ironically he was never charged under the law that bore his name). This original law was struck down as an unconstitutional restriction on First Amendment rights by the Supreme Court in 1991,[2] but like other states California had drafted its own later version with this decision in mind, and its supporters believed that their more carefully worded law would be acceptable to the courts.

Are "Son of Sam" laws just?

Unfortunately for Frank Sinatra Jr., this was not the case. Barry Keenan's petition to the California Supreme Court in February of 2002 was successful, and the Justices unanimously rejected the state's Son of Sam law on free speech grounds. Many traditional supporters of expanded First Amendment rights were pleased by the decision: others were less happy. Just as Senator Jesse Helms had argued that there was a difference between the government's censoring controversial art and its being obliged to finance it with public money, so critics of the California decision said that the right to tell a story did not automatically go hand-in-hand with the privilege of being rewarded for it. As the San Diego Tribune wrote, "There's nothing stopping Keenan, or any other felon, from writing a book or screenplay or musical or whatever . . . but the Constitution does not say that convicted felons like Keenan have a 'right' to be paid for telling their crime stories."[3] Advocates for victims' rights saw the court's decision as a slap in the face for the innocent: those who suffered crime but who were less "newsworthy" appeared to be the losers in a system that ensured that crime

In February of 2002 the California Supreme Court ruled that Barry Keenan, the kidnapper of singing legend Frank Sinatra's son, could not be barred from receiving payment for the movie rights to his story. Victims' rights groups complained that this was a victory for powerful media interests rather than genuine free expression. Here Keenan is shown talking to reporters during the case.

would indeed pay. Were, they asked, the rights at stake here really those of the media, whose only interest was to feed the public's insatiable appetite for lurid true crime stories in a quest for profits?

This case is just one example of the way in which the much-hallowed freedom of the press is abused in the modern United States. The Founding Fathers rightly argued that newspaper editors need to be able to publish without fear of heavy-handed state censorship or the punishment of unpopular ideas: such principles remain important today. But with rights come accompanying responsibilities, and sadly the experience of the past few decades has shown the hugely powerful and influential U.S. media world to be arrogant and exploitative in the use of its liberties—rewarding criminals for their past behavior with tempting contracts, for one. The law needs to be framed to guard genuinely important press freedoms but also recognize that inadequate regulation of the media causes more harm than good, and allows the rights of individual privacy and dignity to be trampled in a ceaseless, cynical rush for "the public's right to know."

> **How is it in the public interest to allow offenders to sell their stories? How is it not?**

Prior restraint is not always unwarranted or unjust.

Prior restraint—sometimes also known as previous restraint—is an important philosophical concept in constitutional law that has special implications for the freedom of the press. When the government enforces prior restraint, it bans the publication or broadcasting of something *before* it is distributed, or sometimes even written or made: it stops a message from being communicated entirely. This is in contrast to "*ex post facto* punishment," where the authorities punish the authors for printing or producing something *after* it has been distributed.

Most people today would accept that prior restraint is a drastic form of government speech control that shouldn't be considered lightly. However, before rejecting it in too knee-jerk a fashion, it is important to consider some of the problems inherent in *ex post facto* punishment. Once something is published, "the cat is out of the bag" and the information has permanently entered the public record (even if the government later tries to suppress it): this means if the speech in question was dangerous, then the damage has already been done. The original issue at the heart of *Near v. Minnesota* (1931), which prohibited prior restraint in the U.S., is a case in point. J.M. Near was a scandal-sheet publisher who owned a virulently anti-Semitic newspaper, *The Saturday Press*, in which he made frequent scurrilous remarks about Minneapolis officials and alleged that a secret Jewish conspiracy was effectively running the city. In response, Minnesota officials banned further publication of the paper, which led to Near's appeal and the historic Supreme Court decision.

FROM THE BENCH

Prior Restraint

Prior restraint of the press was explicitly declared unconstitutional in the *Near v. Minnesota* (1931) decision, which struck down a ban on an anti-Semitic newspaper, *The Saturday Press*. Not all the Justices agreed, however, that the case in question involved a real breach of traditional liberties. Justice Butler was one of three members of the panel who dissented:

> [The stories in *The Saturday Press*] unquestionably constitute an abuse of the right of free press. The statute denounces the things done as a nuisance on the ground, as stated by the state Supreme Court, that they threaten morals, peace, and good order. There is no question of the power of the state to denounce such transgressions. . . . It is well known that existing libel laws are inadequate effectively to suppress evils resulting from the kind of business and publications that are shown in this case.

> —*Near v. State of Minnesota Ex Rel. Olson*, 283 U.S. 697 (1931)

Earlier chapters discussed at some length this kind of "hate speech," and there is no reason here to rehash all the arguments in favor or opposed to its restriction. However, it is worth considering the special role of the press as a transmitter and magnifier of such offensive speech. If a single person makes a hate-filled comment aloud, the damage will inevitably be small no matter what he or she says. But if the same comment is made in a newspaper, it can have a much more virulent effect. Journalists are vastly more influential "speakers" in the marketplace of ideas than are ordinary persons, and their words carry particular weight, particularly on the impressionable. Irresponsible papers like *The Saturday Post* do enormous harm by seeding lies throughout society, and even if *ex post facto* punishment is possible, the injury will often be irreparable. In cases like this, it is better for the community as a whole to accept the difficult burden of prior restraint rather than see press freedoms run amok.

A too-free press can threaten national security.

The case for prior restraint is even greater when it concerns issues of state secrecy and national defense. The dilemma of how to balance respect for freedom of the press with the need to safeguard America's security was starkly highlighted by *The Progressive*'s "H-Bomb" issue in November of 1979.

Early that year the magazine *The Progressive* announced that it would soon publish an article giving a long and detailed description of how a hydrogen bomb worked. The magazine's editors argued that all of the information contained in the article was freely available in the public domain, and that they were publishing it in order to increase awareness about nuclear disarmament issues. The government, which had been tipped off about the upcoming article by a concerned scientist, asked a federal

> If the *Progressive* case had reached the Supreme Court, which way would the decision probably have gone?

judge to issue a restraining order preventing the issue of *The Progressive* in question from being published. Justice Robert Warren of the Wisconsin District Court agreed to this, saying that even if the article's information was theoretically from unrestricted sources, it was still a dangerous way of popularizing sensitive data. Would foreign governments unfriendly to the United States be aided in their nuclear programs by the article, even if only slightly? If so, argued Judge Warren, it was better to use prior restraint than to take such a sinister risk. The magazine appealed the restraining order and it was scheduled for review by the Seventh Circuit federal court, but shortly before the review was due to begin the government, under increasing public criticism for its pursuit of *The Progressive*, dropped its case and the controversy became moot: the article was published that November. Because it never reached the Supreme Court, the *Progressive* affair ended unsatisfactorily for everyone. The government lost its bid to have the article suppressed, but its

FROM THE BENCH

How to Build an H-Bomb

In 1979, amidst great controversy, the magazine *The Progressive* announced the planned publication of an article describing in detail the workings of the hydrogen bomb. Upholding a government request to ban the article's publication, the presiding judge for the Wisconsin District Court wrote:

> This Court can find no plausible reason why the public needs to know the technical details about hydrogen bomb construction to carry on an informed debate on this issue. . . . What is involved here is information dealing with the most destructive weapon in the history of mankind. . . . Faced with a stark choice between upholding the right to continued life and the right to freedom of the press, most jurists would have no difficulty in opting for the chance to continue to breathe.

> —*United States v. Progressive, Inc.*, 467 F. Supp. 990 (1979)

right to issue prior restraint orders was not challenged in the courts either.

In hindsight, it is clear that the *Progressive* H-Bomb article was not a significant threat to U.S. national security. But at the time the case worried even some fellow journalists, who felt that *The Progressive*'s editors were being cavalier about genuine secrecy concerns in a bid to make an empty point about freedom of the press. Twenty years later, and with the terrifying results of terrorist attacks only too fresh in the national memory, the *Progressive* affair has an even more troubling ring to it. In an age in which small terror groups can plot to build weapons of mass destruction, including chemical and biological agents and even nuclear devices, can a nation afford to be puritanical about prior restraint when publications risk aiding its enemies?

> Should the press give "the public" what it wants — content that is exciting and easy to read — or content of a higher academic level?
>
> Does the public really want what critics claim it wants?

Press rights can limit the rights of ordinary citizens.

The damage that the press can do to society is not always directly political. Indeed, it is sometimes caused by the media's obsession with the prurient and the trivial in place of more substantial issues. The major media companies are often criticized as part of a downward-spiraling race to produce the tackiest and least informative books, TV shows, and films possible: to appeal to the mass public's worst instincts and play to "the lowest common denominator."

Crime reporting is a key example. The American press has a long-established right to witness and write up courtroom events. This was intended to make justice in the United States as transparent as possible and to prevent the imposition of secret and unfair trials, a laudable aim in itself. But as was clear during the 1980s and 1990s, this worthy goal has been distorted by the

In recent years the press has been criticized for its excessive interest in high-profile criminal cases, often creating a "media circus" that can be criticized for trivializing and distorting the workings of the judicial system. This came to a head during the O.J. Simpson trial in 1995; here, reporters fight for a glimpse of the occupants of a limousine at the pretrial hearings. But press freedoms can be an important safeguard against injustice, too, and it is for this very reason that the Constitution's "freedom of the press" clause was established.

media circus that sensationalizes exciting courtroom stories without worrying about the effects this might have on justice. Terrible crimes are turned into entertainment, and those involved in the case are subject to merciless hounding by the press—which feels free to speculate endlessly on the possible truth behind the story, regardless of the traumatic emotional effect this might have on the people personally caught up in the ordeal, or on the jurors who are actually going to decide its outcome. No one who watched the O.J. Simpson spectacle unfold on television during the mid-1990s can really deny that the intensive media interest in the case had no influence on the events within the courtroom: indeed, it sometimes seemed as if the attorneys on both sides were making their case more to the waiting news cameras than to the jury. Attempts to counteract the effects of media intrusion, such as sequestering juries for long periods of time away from the attentions of the press, seem doomed to failure if the example of the Simpson trial is to be relied on. If this is the First Amendment at work, it is a curious form of "freedom" that so often puts the interests of media moguls above those of ordinary people.

———————•——————•——————•———————

During the first half of the 20th century, the United States government began to regulate large industries in a previously unheard-of way, because it recognized that the state could not ignore their power to do great harm as well as good in society. The same sort of attitude is appropriate toward the industry that is the 21st-century American media, a conglomerate that undoubtedly performs many important and beneficial roles but which is also capable of causing great mischief. First Amendment rights for the press are just as important now as they were when the Bill of Rights was adopted, but journalists cannot take cover behind the traditional dislike of prior restraint laws every time they behave irresponsibly towards vulnerable members of the community, national security, or the judicial system. It is essential that the United States temper its enthusiasm for freedom of expression in print and on-screen with the acknowledgment that liberties do not come without costs.

> **When is the cost of free speech high enough to warrant restrictions?**

Freedom of the Press Is Vital to a Healthy Democracy

Throughout the 1982–1983 academic year, a group of students enrolled in the Journalism II class at Hazelwood East High School near St. Louis, Missouri, had published a short newspaper, *The Spectrum*, every few weeks as part of their curriculum assignments. When the final issue of the year was completed, the faculty advisor teaching the class left a copy of the galley proofs with the school principal for review, just as he had always done. The principal was not pleased by what he read. Two of the articles in *The Spectrum's* special section on social issues discussed student pregnancy and the effects of parental divorce on children. The principal asked the faculty advisor to remove these articles, and the paper was finally

What are the political and social advantages of a free press? Why did the Framers protect this so specifically?

published in an abridged version.

Some of the student journalists who had worked on the paper, and who were uninformed about the changes until the day of the issue's release, objected to what they saw as administrative censorship. After getting an unsatisfactory answer from their school, they filed suit in federal district court, charging a violation of First Amendment press rights. This initial suit was unsuccessful, but on appeal the circuit court upheld the complaint. Hazelwood School District appealed in turn, and finally in 1988 the case reached the Supreme Court. The Court ruled 5 to 3 that Hazelwood had *not* curtailed its students' civil rights because the First Amendment did not apply to them: the students were involved in official school-sponsored activities (the paper, remember, had been published as part of a journalism class) and as such Hazelwood was entitled to exercise reasonable controls on what the students said or did so long as legitimate educational standards were at stake.[1]

Reaction to the Supreme Court's decision was swift. Civil libertarians complained that the *Hazelwood* ruling effectively stripped public school students of many of their rights of free expression, and gave school authorities far too much discretion in what they could restrict in the name of educational necessity. *Hazelwood* was cited in a number of lower court decisions in which schools were permitted to censor textbooks on grounds of "vulgarity" and punish student council nominees for comments made in their election campaigns. Legislators in California, Massachusetts and several other states successfully introduced press protection bills that gave their public school students the rights that the Supreme Court had denied them.

The *Hazelwood* case illustrates several important, and often overlooked, truths about freedom of the press today. One is that constitutional decisions do not invariably go in favor of the media: despite the stereotype that exists that

American journalists have free rein to do virtually anything with the blessing of the courts, there have been a number of serious reverses for newspapers and broadcasters, with repercussions for the scope of free expression in the public forum. Another point about *Hazelwood* is that press freedom does not simply concern the mass media: ordinary students in schools and colleges are just as affected by the Supreme Court's decisions as are CNN and *The New York Times*, and students need to be aware of the rights and restrictions that pertain to them too. The recent history of First Amendment press rights has not been a particularly happy one. In concentrating only on the media's occasional excesses and biases—and there *is* an unfortunate reality behind some of these criticisms—the public has tended to ignore the key role that a free press still plays in the democratic life of America. Zeal to condemn exploitative and salacious journalism must not destroy the liberties that have been so important in keeping the nation informed and alert to abuses of power.

FROM THE BENCH

Dissent in *Hazelwood*

In *Hazelwood School District v. Kuhlmeier* (1988), the Supreme Court ruled that it was acceptable for public school authorities to exercise prior restraint on student-run newspapers. Still, some of the Justices disagreed with the logic behind the decision. Justice Brennan dissented:

> When the young men and women of Hazelwood East High School registered for Journalism II, they expected a civics lesson. . . . In my view the principal broke more than just a promise. He violated the First Amendment's prohibitions against censorship of any student expression that neither disrupts classwork nor invades the rights of others, and against any censorship that is not narrowly tailored to serve its purpose.

> —*Hazelwood School District v. Kuhlmeier*, 484 U.S. 260 (1988)

Media scrutiny of the government should not be curtailed.

One of the greatest tests of the delicate balance between the freedom of the press and the need for state secrecy came with the Pentagon Papers affair in 1971. This was in fact the first time in U.S. history that the federal government had ever attempted to use a court injunction to exercise prior restraint on a publication: its outcome was therefore of crucial importance for the future direction of First Amendment liberties.

The case began when scientist Daniel Ellsberg allegedly gave a copy of a confidential government document that he had helped write to *The New York Times* and *The Washington Post*. The document, the Pentagon Papers, was a secret (and highly critical) history of America's diplomatic and military involvement in the Vietnam conflict, which was then at its height and the subject of great controversy in the United States. As soon as both newspapers began publishing copies

The Pentagon Papers

The battle over the publication of leaked government documents by *The New York Times* and *The Washington Post* in 1971 was a critical moment in the relationship between the free press and the state. Author David Rudenstine summarized the Supreme Court's decision to overrule the government in his book on the affair, *The Day the Presses Stopped*:

> The Court decided to risk the dangers inherent in a free press because the alternative resolution—enhancing government power to censor the press—was even more threatening to a stable and vital democracy. This was a courageous decision supportive of the public's right to be informed about important public affairs.
>
> —Rudenstine, p. 355

of the Pentagon Papers in serialized form, the Justice Department petitioned federal district judges in New York and Washington to temporarily restrain any further extracts. The courts in each jurisdiction came up with contrary decisions, New York confirming the restraint and Washington refusing it, and so the Supreme Court immediately stepped in to resolve what was clearly a major constitutional issue. Postponing its normal summer recess, the Court reviewed the conflicting decisions and in a complicated six-to-three vote threw out the prior restraint requests on the grounds that the government had not provided sufficient evidence that national security was at stake.

Were the two Pentagon Papers decisions—*New York Times v. United States* (1971)[2] and *United States v. Washington Post* (1971)[3]—victories for the free press, then? In some ways, yes: publication of the serialized document continued, and the government was thwarted in its attempt to censor the two newspapers. On the other hand, the Supreme Court's rulings were very unclear as to whether future prior restraint injunctions would be constitutionally valid or not. Many legal observers felt that the Court had missed a crucial opportunity to clarify once and for all the status of journalistic freedom in sensitive matters of state. However, the Pentagon Papers had at least to some degree confirmed the right of newspapers to conduct probing reports free from state interference, and the importance of this right became even clearer just a couple of years later when two reporters from *The Washington Post*, Bob Woodward and Carl Bernstein, investigated a series of wrongdoings involving high-level government officials—the Watergate affair—that ultimately brought down Richard Nixon's presidency. Without the guarantee of a free press, Woodward and Bernstein's shocking revelations might never have made it into the public sphere.

> **What would have happened if the *Times* and the *Post* had lost the Pentagon Papers cases?**

The intense media scrutiny of the private life of President Clinton, which led to Clinton's unsuccessful 1998 impeachment by Congress on perjury charges, highlighted the close relationship between a free press and American politics. Independent Counsel Kenneth Starr became a hero or villain to millions of TV viewers and newspaper readers during the investigation and for the lurid details of the Starr Report; here, an anti-Starr protestor vents his anger.

The press suffers too many restrictions in the courts.

One of the other tensions between journalism and the effective workings of the state comes from newspaper and TV coverage of courtroom cases. The Constitution guarantees all accused citizens a fair trial, and some skeptics argue that this clashes with the constitutional right to freedom of the press—and in some cases ought to override it. But there is no necessary contradiction between these two rights; media coverage actually adds to the likelihood of a fair trial. Unfortunately, not all judges agree with this, and there is an additional complication when journalists are privy to confidential information that might affect the outcome of a trial: does their right to keep the identity of their sources secret outweigh the importance of courtroom justice?

The ability of judges to directly censor news reports of trials—often known as "gag orders"—was severely limited by a 1975 Supreme Court decision in which the Nebraska Press Association successfully appealed a prior restraint order issued by a state judge during a preliminary criminal hearing.[4] In that decision, the Court decreed that judges could authorize such gags on the media only if there was a compelling case that press coverage would make a fair trial impossible (by, say, prejudicing the potential jury pool against the defendant in advance). Since it is very difficult for judges to produce such overwhelming evidence in favor of a gag, they have largely abandoned attempts to directly limit press coverage. However, there is a loophole in the 1976 decision: while judges may no longer gag reporters with

Gag Orders

In recent years, many courtroom journalists have been subject to legal obstacles, such as judicial "gag orders" forbidding certain people involved in criminal cases from speaking publicly. The Reporters Committee for Freedom of the Press (RCFP), an advocacy group for journalists, is concerned about this development:

> Courts routinely impose gag orders to limit public discussion about pending cases, presuming that there is no better way to ensure a fair trial. Many judges fear that having cameras in courtrooms will somehow interfere with the decorum and solemnity of judicial proceedings. Such steps . . . may actually harm the integrity of a trial because court secrecy and limits on information are contrary to the fundamental constitutional guarantee of a public trial.

—www.rcfp.org/secretjustice/gagorders/series.html

ease, they *can* gag specific participants in the trial from speaking to the press—an indirect form of control which effectively prevents journalists from covering trial stories properly. Such redirected gag orders are increasingly common, and advocacy groups like The Reporters Committee for Freedom of the Press have complained that there is a creeping growth of prior restraint in America's courtrooms.

What happens when an investigative reporter who has gained important information about a criminal case from a confidential source is asked to name that source in the courtroom? If journalists reveal this information, they may be temporarily aiding the course of justice but they will also be undermining the guarantee of confidentiality between the media and its sources, which in the long run could harm the press's ability to uncover public wrongdoing. And if journalists defy the judge's demand that they uncover source information in their testimony, they can be found in contempt of court and imprisoned.

The Supreme Court provided some constitutional guidance on this issue in *Branzburg v. Hayes* (1972), in which it recognized a qualified privilege of source confidentiality for journalists: the government can only demand testimony when the information is of compelling relevance to the case and there are no other means of obtaining it.[5] Because this protection is rather weak, however, some individual states have passed "shield laws" that give journalists additional rights to keep their sources confidential. But the ever-present threat of imprisonment still acts as a serious restraint on many reporters working in America today.

> Are shield laws a good idea? What are the parallels among a reporter with a confidential source, a lawyer with a client, and a priest with a parishioner? What are the important differences?

The press is "a necessary irritant."

Because the public has grown increasingly disillusioned with the mass media in the past few decades, there have been suggestions that new ways should be found to "balance" allegedly biased press coverage. Some of the wilder excesses of intrusive and arrogant media coverage are to blame for this backlash, and it's unfortunate that newspapers and television have, to some extent, brought this resentment onto themselves. The problem with legal corrections to the untrammeled freedom of the press, however, is that the cures are frequently worse than the original disease. In trying to suppress some of the more obnoxious tendencies of the media, the U.S. may end up putting limits on its important constitutional role of informing the people.

Libel law involving public officials is a case in point. In March of 1960, at the height of the civil rights campaign in the segregated southern states, *The New York Times* published an advertisement paid for by a campaigning civil rights group that made some comments about police behavior in Montgomery, Alabama. Although he was not specifically mentioned in the advertisement, L.B. Sullivan, one of the former commissioners of public affairs in Montgomery objected to some factual errors about the police department he had helped supervise, and he sued the newspaper for defamation. An Alabama jury awarded Sullivan $500,000 in damages, a decision that was confirmed by

The Danger of Public Cynicism About the Media

There has been a backlash of public mistrust against the mass media since the pioneering free press cases of the 1970s, but as Bruce Sanford, an expert on privacy and libel law, argues in his book *Don't Shoot the Messenger*, too much cynicism may obscure the very important work that the media still does in protecting civil liberties:

First Amendment freedoms should not depend so much on the public's approval of the press's work, or on the press performing public service, as on the recognition that as awful as they may behave at times, we are much better off relying on them than on government for our liberties.

—Sanford, p. 194

the state's supreme court. Although it was true that *The New York Times* had unwittingly published falsehoods about the Montgomery police, the Alabama decision was a serious threat because of the "chilling effect" it would have on subsequent press discussion of public issues: if government officials could sue newspapers for large sums of money whenever they made errors of fact, it would dissuade the media from tackling controversial issues at all. Fortunately, the Supreme Court overturned the decision in a 1964 ruling, *New York Times v. Sullivan*.[6] They decreed that public officials could only sue the press for libel if there was "actual malice" involved in the misstatement—in other words, if the newspaper had known in advance that it was making errors of fact but had gone ahead regardless. The *Sullivan* ruling was a welcome protection against what could have become a major barrier to a free press.

The working of a free press has never been perfect. But if one wants to see an example of a "responsible," impeccably behaved media, one only needs to look at the trim and prudent output of the Soviet Union's official paper, *Pravda*, and the other newspaper organizations of Communist Eastern Europe in the 1970s and 1980s, forever pushing "upbeat" stories and never stepping out of line. However unpleasant the American media might sometimes be—and the nation should be constantly pushing for more substantive, mature journalism from American news publishers and broadcasters—it is still better to allow lapses of taste and good judgment if the alternative is the stifling of public debate. Attempts to bridle the press usually do more harm to democracy than good: for better or worse, journalists are among the most effective guardians in the defense of justice and truth.

How reliable are newspapers and other members of the mass media?

What damage might they cause through errors of fact?

The Current
Challenges to
Free Speech

The issues discussed in this volume represent only a small
fraction of the First Amendment controversies that are
being debated in the United States today. Freedom of speech is a
vast topic with almost limitless possibilities and points of honest
disagreement, and it is unlikely that any common consensus
about the "correct" interpretation of the right to free expression
will come about soon. The remaining portion of this book will
look at just a few of the other First Amendment topics that are
likely to be in the headlines in the immediate future.

Terrorism and Free Speech

By far the most serious threat to American security in the
early 21st century must be that of international terrorism.
The devastating attacks in New York and Washington, D.C. on
September 11, 2001 made it clear how vulnerable the United

States can be to aggression from extremist groups operating within as well as beyond American borders, and the need for the government to act swiftly and effectively to protect citizens from other terrorist outrages. Part of the fallout from the 9/11 attacks has been an increasing tension between constitutional liberties on the one hand, and on the other the authorities' responsibility to investigate and prevent future incidents of terrorist activity. Freedom of speech rights have been among the casualties in this rush to preempt terrorism; and some people feel that their rights to patriotic expression have been curtailed in a corresponding overreaction against offending people of different races or nationalities.

For example, in the months since 9/11, groups like the National Coalition Against Censorship (NCAC) have catalogued a growing number of complaints about restrictions on free speech, either by government authorities or private organizations.[1] These range from the White House's request that the news media not carry videotaped messages allegedly recorded by Al Qaeda terrorists like Osama bin Laden, to prohibitions on the wearing of American flag badges in college libraries for reasons of "sensitivity." The heightened emotional atmosphere across the nation since the destruction of the World Trade Center towers and the attack on the Pentagon has, according to NCAC, had a chilling effect on First Amendment liberties both for supporters and for critics of the current administration. Censorship of some kind is virtually inevitable during wartime, but what happens when the "war" has no clear boundaries or end date? If, as White House spokesman Ari Fleischer has said, are there "reminders to all Americans that they need to watch what they say" in a time of crisis, will the hard-fought freedoms of the First Amendment survive intact?[2]

Free Speech in Mass Entertainment
Restrictions and First Amendment questions have always plagued the mass entertainment media, which tend to reflect

FROM THE BENCH

The Right to Denounce the Government

Whitney v. California was one of several important cases to emerge from the "Red Scare"—the fear of Communism—that followed World War I. Whitney was accused of collaborating with the Communist Labor Party in violation of a California law against "criminal syndicalism"—organizing support for groups that threaten violence or other illegal activities. In his concurring opinion, Justice Brandeis discussed the requirements for state-imposed restrictions on political speech and free assembly. He argued that in order for state intervention to be justified, a danger to the government must be shown that is "clear," "imminent" or "present," and "serious"—that is, citizens or groups must be free to advocate, for example, the violent overthrow of the government, *unless* they evince a clear intention of when and how this is to be done and the effect of the planned action would be serious enough to warrant intervention. In the words of Justice Brandeis:

> Fear of serious injury cannot alone justify suppression of free speech and assembly. Men feared witches and burnt women. It is the function of speech to free men from the bondage of irrational fears. To justify suppression of free speech there must be reasonable ground to fear that serious evil will result if free speech is practiced. There must be reasonable ground to believe that the danger apprehended is imminent. There must be reasonable ground to believe that the evil to be prevented is a serious one....
>
> [E]ven advocacy of violation [of a law], however reprehensible morally, is not a justification for denying free speech where the advocacy falls short of incitement and there is nothing to indicate that the advocacy would be immediately acted on. The wide difference between advocacy and incitement, between preparation and attempt, between assembling and conspiracy, must be borne in mind....

—*Whitney v. California,* 274 U.S. 357 (1927)

the interests of the young, who in turn tend to rebel against the morals of the old. (Ed Sullivan called Elvis Presley "unfit for a family audience" in 1956, and the Beatles were denounced for their shaggy hair.) Of course, any speech act that seeks to entertain in a non-traditional way will draw criticism from those who hold traditional values. Hollywood has been regulated by the notoriously repressive Hays Code, the ineffectual Legion of Decency, or the imperfect MPAA rating system since the 1930s, but the mainstream now seems to have settled comfortably into the MPAA ratings and tends to leave the edgiest material to independent films. (Many independent films will star "crossover" actors, who seek refuge in riskier work when their mainstream personas limit their artistic expression.) "Banned books" are no longer as much of an issue in education as they once were, and now an annual Banned Books Week, sponsored in part by the American Library Association, has become a celebration of intellectual freedom.

> **Is America stronger or weaker for having strong First Amendment liberties?**

The largest issue now is that of labeling—the extension of the MPAA's successful rating system to other media. Labels have been applied to music since the famous "parental advisory" stickers came into being in 1985, and now they appear on television programs, Internet sites, and adult print media, some even stating precisely what in the product may cause offense. Regulations are still in place, too, as to what can be said or shown on television at given hours. But doubts have often been raised about the result of labeling; an example is the backfiring of the X rating in film, which by 1990 had become a compelling reason to see the films it meant to restrict. The recent trend in the mass entertainment media has been toward self-censorship, and artists (notably in hip-hop) are

> **Which current film stars are "typecast"— cast in the same kinds of role all the time?**
>
> **Would taking on edgier roles damage their careers?**

regulating their own content so as to avoid regulation from the outside. As long as there is labeling, though, there must be someone present to ensure that the labels lead to action, so the system is widely criticized as comforting but ineffective. The current frontier in this question is undoubtedly video games, especially with regard to violence and sexuality.

Free Speech and the Internet

Terrorism's effect on Internet free speech—including the closing of websites with alleged terrorist links, and the removal of information from government portals that could be potentially useful to terrorists—have been among the most visible signs of the new post–9/11 atmosphere. But cyberspace raises peculiar First Amendment problems of its own, because its international character belies traditional state attempts to regulate speech: there is no tangible distinction between a purely "American," constitutionally protected Internet zone, and the rest. This means that individuals, companies, and organizations operating within cyberspace have little clear direction as to what

FROM THE BENCH

The End of the Communications Decency Act

In *Reno v. ACLU* (1997) the Supreme Court confirmed an earlier Pennsylvania court decision that the 1996 Communications Decency Act was unconstitutional. Justice Stevens wrote the majority opinion:

> The record demonstrates that the growth of the Internet has been and continues to be phenomenal. As a matter of constitutional tradition, in the absence of evidence to the contrary, we presume that governmental regulation of the content of speech is more likely to interfere with the free exchange of ideas than to encourage it. The interest in encouraging freedom of expression in a democratic society outweighs any theoretical but unproven benefit of censorship.

> —*Reno v. American Civil Liberties Union (ACLU)*, 521 U.S. 844 (1997)

free expression rules apply to them, or what effect foreign government regulations may have on their speech.

One of the most striking examples of this clash between government prerogatives and Internet free speech happened in 1995, when Munich police ordered that the German subsidiary of the Internet service provider CompuServe suspend over 200 newsgroups because of their allegedly offensive content.[3] Since there was no technical way that CompuServe could remove these groups in Germany alone, it chose to strip them completely from the Internet rather than defy the local ban. In effect, Internet users in places like the United States—where much of the newsgroup content in question was perfectly legal and constitutionally protected—were being forbidden from accessing certain speech because of the decisions of a government thousands of miles away. CompuServe's chief executive in Germany was even given a suspended prison sentence for "distributing pornography," and the company spoke for a time of abandoning operations in Germany entirely as the only way to resolve the issue. Eventually, most of the newsgroups under the ban were returned to the Internet, and the case inspired attempts to reach multinational agreement on the liabilities incurred by service providers like CompuServe. But it seems that, as cyberspace becomes an even more important forum for expression, there will have to be a new legal paradigm transcending old notions of speech and nationality.

> Given that the Internet cannot be contained within the borders of any one country, what rights should an Internet user have? How should these be decided?
>
> Can Americans trust their constitutional rights to protect them online?

Political Correctness

Throughout most of the First Amendment's history, challenges to speech have tended to come from the more traditional, conservative wing of American politics, either because of alleged indecency, or irreverence, or threats to national security. From the late 1980s onwards, however, a loose left-of-center ideology described by its critics as "political correctness" (PC) began to make headlines, as did complaints that "language police," particularly in schools and colleges, were permitting or forbidding certain types of words on ideological grounds. The ill-fated attempt to create campus speech codes, described earlier in this book, was the most notorious example of this kind of PC regulation, which novelist Saul Bellow defined as "free speech without debate." However, some liberals charged that the PC scare was largely an invention of conservatives who were trying to demonize the legitimate proscription of insensitive language, and falsely imply that there was a wholesale, organized censorship policy in effect in the United States. They argued that the political Right used its own form of PC—"patriotic correctness"—in condemning free speech that wasn't to its liking.

The conflict came to a head in the battle over the Smithsonian National Air and Space Museum's 1995 exhibit on the *Enola Gay*, the B-29 bomber that dropped the atomic bomb on Hiroshima in August of 1945, helping to end the Second World War.[4] The original plan for the exhibit was to include a very large range of photos and commentary on the effects as well as the planning of the Enola Gay's fateful mission, with some gruesome images of the devastation wrought by the A-Bomb. When Congressional conservatives found out about the exhibit they complained bitterly that the Air and Space Museum was adopting "revisionist," un-American history, and they demanded formal hearings into the conduct of the Smithsonian and the future of its $300 million budget. Faced with this barrage of criticism the Museum agreed to drastically pare down the Enola Gay exhibit, removing all potentially offensive elements as well as reviewing other upcoming exhibits that might prove politically controversial. The outcome was viewed very differently by the opposing sides: conservatives believed that they had won an important victory over PC in public education, whereas liberal

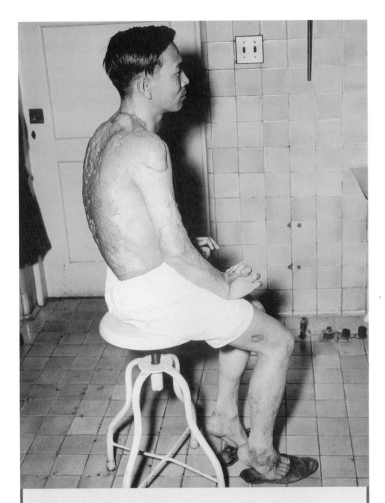

When the Smithsonian National Air and Space Museum announced its plans to host a major exhibition on the dropping of the atomic bombs on Japan—an exhibition that would include graphic images of the effects of the bombing, such as this man's scars—the Museum was subjected to a barrage of criticism as being "politically incorrect." Was the subsequent decision to exclude such images an example of censorship or of good sense? Are censorship and good sense always in opposition?

supporters of the original exhibit claimed that Congress' heavy-handed censorship had interfered with the open discussion of historical issues. The great PC debate continues to haunt First Amendment debate today.

Commercial Speech

Although it does not explicitly say so, it has generally been assumed that the focus of the First Amendment's protection of speech is on *political* expression. This, however, leaves open the question as to what other kinds of speech might be protected under the Constitution. The history of Supreme Court rulings during the last 100 years has shown an increasing willingness to count non-political speech—speech with artistic, literary, scientific, or other merit, for example—as included within First Amendment rights. But the status of commercial speech, particularly that used for advertising purposes, is still not clear.

> **Is it in a nation's interest to emphasize—or only to tell—one side of its history?**
>
> **Which voices are the most important in the story of, for example, Pearl Harbor? Of Hiroshima and Nagasaki? Of the Battle of Orleans?**

In the early decades of the 20th century, Congress reacted to a host of complaints about dishonest and spurious advertising in the popular press by creating federal institutions like the Food and Drug Administration (FDA) and the Federal Trade Commission (FTC) to regulate the advertising world and to punish false and misleading commercial claims. The government's low estimation of First Amendment rights for businesses was apparently confirmed by a 1942 Supreme Court decision, *Valentine v. Chrestensen*, where it ruled that purely commercial advertising was unprotected, and this decision held sway until the 1970s.[5] Then in *Bigelow v. Virginia* (1975), the Court made an important change in direction.[6] The case involved an advertisement in a Charlottesville newspaper that provided information about legal New York abortion clinics: the Managing

Editor of the paper was convicted of breaking a Virginia state ordinance that forbade the dissemination of advertisements about abortion. The Court decreed for the first time that advertisements "of potential interest and value" to the general public *were* constitutionally protected, although they made it clear that false or deceptive advertising remained punishable. Later Supreme Court decisions expanded this new ruling slightly, although they still afforded commercial speech a much lower level of protection than political expression. Since Bigelow, business advocates have pressed for the greater extension of First Amendment rights into the commercial world: the recent controversy over whether e-mail "spam" can be lawfully regulated by the government is one of new commercial issues raised by the growth of the Internet.

> **Is commercial speech as important as political or artistic speech?**
>
> **What can be done about spam?**

Campaign Finance Reform

Public cynicism about the effects of huge cash contributions on American political campaigns has fueled the drive towards new regulations and restrictions on the financing of elections. However, this cuts across the traditional interpretation of "money = speech" held by the Supreme Court, making such attempts to ban types of campaign contribution an issue of free expression. The controversy has created strange alliances: The ACLU—which is in favor of public financing of campaigns, but believes most of the recent legislation on the problem to be unconstitutional—has found itself in league with conservative lobbyists like the National Rifle Association (NRA) and the anti-abortion National Right to Life Committee. What these unlikely political bedfellows share in common is a belief that too strict a form of campaign financing will inhibit their ability to speak out on issues of national importance.

The Supreme Court has not provided especially clear

guidance. In *Buckley v. Valeo* (1976) it decided that contributions from individual donors to a campaign could be capped at a fixed dollar amount, but that campaign expenditure as a whole could not be limited.[7] Twenty years later, in *Colorado Republican Federal Campaign Committee v. Federal Election Commission* (1996), the Court decreed that political parties and lobbyists could spend unlimited amounts on election campaigns so long as they did not directly coordinate their spending plans with the candidates themselves.[8] But the Justices were widely divided on the issue, a minority dissenting from the decision and arguing that more spending caps were necessary—while two of the majority Justices went in the opposite direction and suggested that *no* government restriction of campaign finance should be countenanced. As of yet there is little real consensus as to the relationship between big-money politics and the First Amendment. What do these issues suggest about the future of American free speech?

Which are the most important issues of free speech today?

Does it seem that all the major First Amendment cases are headed in the same direction?

How might the composition of the Supreme Court help to explain this—or is it more a factor of the changing U.S. population, or of technology, or of the world community?

One trend to notice is the steady breakdown in the separation between *authors* and *readers* that is being accelerated by the growth of such media as the Internet. As self-publishing becomes an ever more common form of personal expression through the cheap and simple means of constructing websites, posting newsgroup messages, and sending e-mail, more and more people will be concerned with their rights not simply as members of a passive audience but also as active writers and contributors to public debate. Most of America is "the press" now, in one way or another, and First Amendment issues such as prior restraint—which at one time would not have figured very prominently in the lives of ordinary people—will become more and more significant to the mass of amateur journalists now coming into existence in cyberspace.

To some extent, however, the longer-term future of the First Amendment will also depend on the composition of the Supreme Court. Interpretive tastes change, partly depending on the general climate of the times but also because of the political leanings of the Justices appointed to the Court. The constitutional history of the 20th century was one of the extension and entrenchment of the rights of ordinary citizens to speak in as many ways as possible; modern Americans have a much broader belief in the scope of the First Amendment now than their predecessors did a century ago. This tendency could continue, or the U.S. might just as easily see a contraction in the boundaries of free speech. The choice of direction, one that will certainly influence your adult life, may be set by the men and women appointed to the Supreme Court bench in the next few years. Judicial choices like these are not simply dry, abstract news stories with no relevance to ordinary people: they affect *you*—in ways that cannot be easily foreseen, perhaps, but which are no less important for all that. So be an active citizen: use the priceless resources given to you by your First Amendment, and keep yourself informed about changes in constitutional law as they come about. Speech will remain truly free only while there are people to listen, think, and respond.

Free Speech and the First Amendment

1 Quoted in "Student Web Sites Pose Rising Test of Free Speech Rights," *The Los Angeles Times*, March 6, 2001.

2 Letter to James Madison, March 15, 1789.

3 *Schenck v. United States*, 249 U.S. 47 (1919).

4 *Schenck v. United States*, 249 U.S. 47 (1919).

5 *Brandenburg v. Ohio*, 395 U.S. 444 (1969).

6 *Near v. State of Minnesota Ex Rel. Olson*, 283 U.S. 697 (1931).

Point: Some Ideas Are Dangerous Enough to Merit Restriction

1 *National Socialist Party v. Skokie*, 432 U.S. 43 (1977).

2 *Smith v. Collin*, 439 U.S. 916 (1978).

3 Available online at *www.fbi.gov/ucr/cius_00/hate00.pdf*.

4 Evelyn Beatrice Hall, *The Friends of Voltaire* (1906). This quotation is often misattributed to Voltaire himself and is in fact modified from Hall. Hall claimed that she was paraphrasing Voltaire's *Traité sur la tolérance*, but she probably had in mind a sentence from Voltaire to a correspondent, here translated loosely: "I disagree profoundly with your ideas but I would give my life for your right to express them." (Letter to M. le Riche, February 6, 1770)

5 *Chaplinsky v. State of New Hampshire*, 315 U.S. 568 (1942).

6 *Halter v. Nebraska*, 205 U.S. 34 (1907).

7 These are discussed in Foerstal, p. 102.

8 Quoted in "Don't Claim Terroristic Cross-Burning Is Protected Speech," *The Houston Chronicle*, June 1, 2002.

Counterpoint: Banning Dangerous Speech Won't Solve the Problem

1 See "Racist Slur Puts Brigitte Bardot in Court Again," *The Independent* (London), January 18, 1998.

2 See "Neo-Nazi Website Stays Ahead of Law." *The Irish Times* (Dublin), August 9, 2002.

3 *Cohen v. California*, 403 U.S. 15 (1971).

4 Quoted at *www.bccla.org/othercontent/00freespeech.html*.

5 Quoted at *users.rcn.com/kyp/schools/bennet2.html*.

6 Quoted at *users.rcn.com/kyp/schools/bennet2.html*.

Point: Obscene Expression Should Not Be Protected

1 See "Obscenity Pledge Voided," *The Los Angeles Times*, January 10, 1991.

2 See "NEA to Pay 4 Denied Arts Grants," *The Washington Post*, June 5, 1993.

3 See "Cincinnati Jury Acquits Museum in Mapplethorpe Obscenity Case," *The New York Times*, October 6, 1990.

4 *Miller v. California*, 413 U.S. 15 (1973).

5 *Jacobellis v. Ohio*, 378 U.S. 184 (1964).

6 Quoted in "Coalition to File Suit Over Internet Rules," *The Washington Post*, February 26, 1996.

7 See *www.wired.com/news/print/0,1294,51544,00.html*.

Counterpoint: Government Should Not Decide What Is Obscene

1 Quoted in "Lenny Bruce Still Testing the Limits," *USA Today*, November 2, 2000.

2 *Joseph Burstyn, Inc. v. Wilson*, 343 U.S. 495 (1952).

3 *Epperson v. Arkansas*, 393 U.S. 97 (1968).

4 *Miller v. California*, 413 U.S. 15 (1973).

5 *Roth v. United States*, 354 U.S. 476 (1957).

6 See "Judge Limits New Law Curbing Internet Speech," *The San Francisco Chronicle*, February 16, 1996.

7 Quoted at *www.efa.org.au/Publish/PR960613.html*.

Point: The "Freedom of the Press" Should Be Restricted

1 See "Sinatra Jr. Tries to Stop Kidnappers' Film Rights," *The Chicago Sun-Times*, August 14, 1998.

2 *Simon & Schuster v. Crime Victims Bd.*, 502 U.S. 105 (1991).

3 Quoted in "Cash for Crime; Ex-con Challenges State's 'Son of Sam' Law," *The San Diego Union-Tribune*, December 10, 2001.

Counterpoint: Freedom of the Press Is Vital to a Healthy Democracy

1 *Hazelwood School District v. Kuhlmeier*, 484 U.S. 260 (1988).

2 *New York Times Co. v. United States*, 403 U.S. 713 (1971).

3 *United States v. Washington Post Co.*, 403 U.S. 943 (1971).

4 *Nebraska Press Association v. Stuart*, 423 U.S. 1027 (1975).

5 *Branzburg v. Hayes*, 408 U.S. 665 (1972).

6 *New York Times Co. v. Sullivan*, 376 U.S. 254 (1964).

The Current Challenges to Free Speech

1 See *www.ncac.org/issues/freeex911.html*.

2 Quoted in "White House Sees Red Over Maher's Remarks," *Daily News* (New York), September 27, 2001.

3 See "Germany Forces Online Service to Censor Internet," *The Los Angeles Times*, December 29, 1995.

4 See "Smithsonian Scales Back Exhibit of B-29 in Atomic Bomb Attack," *The New York Times*, January 31, 1995.

5 *Valentine v. Chrestensen*, 316 U.S. 52 (1942).

6 *Bigelow v. Virginia*, 421 U.S. 809 (1975).

7 *Buckley v. Valeo*, 424 U.S. 1 (1976).

8 *Colorado Republican Federal Campaign Committee, et al. v. Federal Election Commission*, 518 U.S. 604 (1996).

General

One of the most important organizations involved in First Amendment policy is the American Civil Liberties Union, or ACLU (*www.aclu.org*). The ACLU not only campaigns on free speech issues but has itself been a litigant in many key Supreme Court cases, such as for example the *Skokie* controversy. Other organizations that campaign for an extension of First Amendment rights include the National Campaign for Freedom of Expression (*www.ncfe.net*), the National Coalition Against Censorship (*www.ncac.org*) and the Office for Intellectual Freedom (*www.ala.org/alaorg/oif/*). Organizations presenting a more conservative attitude towards free speech include the American Family Association (*www.afa.net*) and the Eagle Forum (*www.eagleforum.org*).

Other useful books on freedom of speech include the following:

Currie, David. *The Constitution of the United States: A Primer for the People.* University of Chicago Press, 2000.

Foerstal, Herbert. *Free Expression and Censorship in America: An Encyclopedia.* Greenwood, 1997.

Gilfoyle, Timothy. "The Moral Origins of Political Surveillance: The Preventive Society in New York City, 1867–1918." *American Quarterly* 38:4 (Autumn 1986): 637.

Hall, Kermit, ed. *By and For the People: Constitutional Rights in American History.* Harlan Davidson, 1991.

Hentoff, Nat. *First Freedom: A Tumultuous History of Free Speech in America.* Delacorte Press, 1980.

Kennedy, Sheila, ed. *Free Expression in America: A Documentary History.* Greenwood, 1999.

Tedford, Thomas. *Freedom of Speech in the United States.* McGraw Hill, 1993.

Hate Speech

The Anti-Defamation League (*www.adl.org*) is one of the principal monitors of extremist speech in the United States, and its extensive website includes a great deal of information about the problem. Books specifically on hate speech include:

Delgado, Richard, and Jean Stefanic. *Must We Defend Nazis?* New York University Press, 1997.

Golding, Martin. *Free Speech on Campus.* Rowman & Littlefield, 2000.

Goldstein, Robert. *Flag Burning and Free Speech: The Case of* Texas v. Johnson. University Press of Kansas, 2000.

Lederer, Laura, and Richard Delgado, eds. *The Price We Pay.* Hill and Wang, 1994.

Walker, Samuel. *Hate Speech: The History of an American Controversy.* University of Nebraska Press, 1994.

Obscenity

The debate over obscenity and the First Amendment has in recent years focused intensely on the Internet and the legal repercussions of its rapid growth. The Electronic Frontier Foundation (*www.eff.org*) is a forum for discussing cyberspace censorship and contains news and updates on free speech issues online. Books specifically on obscenity law include these:

Kolbert, Kathryn. *Censoring the Web: Leading Advocates Debate Today's Most Controversial Issues.* New Press, 2001.

Mackey, Thomas. *Pornography on Trial: A Handbook with Cases, Laws, and Documents.* ABC-CLIO, 2002.

Peck, Robert. *Libraries, the First Amendment, and Cyberspace: What You Need to Know.* American Library Association, 2000.

Freedom of the Press

There are a number of different organizations representing either journalists or readers which take strong positions on the question of the freedom of the press. Internet sites of particular interest include Accuracy in Media (*www.aim.org*), Fairness and Accuracy in Reporting (*www.fair.org*), and the Reporters Committee for Freedom of the Press (*www.rcfp.org*). Books specifically on the press and the First Amendment include the following, respectively the story of the Pentagon Papers and a defense of the media:

Rudenstine, David. *The Day the Presses Stopped.* University of California Press, 1996.

Sanford, Bruce. *Don't Shoot the Messenger.* The Free Press, 1999.

Legislation and Case Law

The Sedition Act of 1798

A very important early attempt to set limits on free speech; imposed fines and imprisonment for speech against the government. Heavily criticized but never actually ruled unconstitutional; it expired automatically after a few years and was never challenged in the Supreme Court.

The Comstock Act (1873)

Criminalized the dissemination through the mail system of information about contraception. Courts permitted doctors to prescribe contraceptives in 1936, and the prohibition on birth control was removed entirely in 1971, though some portions of the act remain in effect.

The Espionage Act (1917) and the Sedition Act of 1918

The latter was in fact an amendment to the former; these were part of a major attempt by the government (under Woodrow Wilson) to curtail free speech rights during the hysteria surrounding World War I.

Schenck v. United States, 249 U.S. 47 (1919)

Established the "clear and present danger" standard for restrictions on speech content; source of the Holmes aphorism about shouting "fire" in a crowded theater.

Near v. Minnesota, 283 U.S. 697 (1931)

Established for the first time in American law that prior restraint is usually unconstitutional.

Chaplinsky v. State of New Hampshire, 315 U.S. 568 (1942)

Introduced the concept of "fighting words" to First Amendment issues.

New York Times v. Sullivan, 376 U.S. 254 (1964)

Established protection from libel suits from public officials except when libel is committed knowingly and maliciously.

Brandenburg v. Ohio, 395 U.S. 444 (1969)

Established the "imminent lawless action" rule for restrictions on speech content.

New York Times Co. v. United States, 403 U.S. 713 (1971)

Ruled (along with the similar *United States v. Washington Post* case) that the injunction against publication of the Pentagon Papers was unlawful.

Cohen v. California, 403 U.S. 15 (1971)

Ruled that offensive speech (but not "fighting words") is constitutionally protected.

Branzburg v. Hayes, 408 U.S. 665 (1972)

Created a qualified right of confidentiality of sources for the media.

Miller v. California, 413 U.S. 15 (1973)

Established the foundations of modern obscenity law.

Nebraska Press Association v. Stuart, 423 U.S. 1027 (1975)
Limited court-ordered "gag orders" on the press.

National Socialist Party v. Skokie, 432 U.S. 43 (1977)
Threw out bans on public marches by politically extreme groups.

Hazelwood School District v. Kuhlmeier, 484 U.S. 260 (1988)
Public schools can restrict the content of school newspapers if the restrictions are "reasonably related" to educational goals.

Texas v. Johnson, 491 U.S. 397 (1989)
Ruled (along with similar case *United States v. Eichman*) that burning the American flag is constitutionally protected.

Simon & Schuster v. Crime Victims Bd., 502 U.S. 105 (1991)
Threw out "Son of Sam" laws prohibiting former criminals from selling their stories to the press.

The Communications Decency Act (CDA, 1996)
The two most controversial provisions of the CDA aimed to protect minors from harmful Internet content: one criminalized "knowing" transmission of anything "obscene or indecent" to anyone under 18 and the other anything "patently offensive as measured by contemporary community standards." Struck down unanimously by the Supreme Court in *Reno v. ACLU* in 1997.

Child Pornography Prevention Act of 1996 (CPPA)
Added "virtual" or "morphed child pornography" to definition of child pornography—images that appear to include children but in fact do not.

Reno, et al. v. American Civil Liberties Union, et al., 521 U.S. 844 (1997)
In a unanimous decision, ruled the two key provisions of the CDA unconstitutional too broad—not "narrowly tailored" enough to restrict only the kinds of speech they meant to restrict—and therefore violations of the First Amendment.

The Children's Online Privacy Protection Act of 1998 (COPPA)
Prohibited commerce in the personal information of children (under 13 years of age) without "verifiable parental consent."

The Child Online Protection Act (COPA or CDA 2, 1998)
Intended as a replacement of the thrown-out CDA provisions. Criminalized the commercial transmission of any material deemed "harmful to minors." Was struck down by *Ashcroft v. ACLU* in 2002.

The Children's Internet Protection Act (CIPA, 2000)
Compelled public libraries and schools to install filtering software on their public-access computer terminals, with the intent of blocking the receipt by minors of inappropriate Internet content, in order to receive vital federal funding. Thrown out by the *ALA v. United States* ruling in May of 2002.

American Library Association (ALA) v. United States, Nos. 01-CV-1303, 01-CV-1322 (E.D. Pa. May 31, 2002), *petition for cert. filed* Sept. 6, 2002 (No. 02-361) Challenged CIPA; a federal court in May of 2002 declared two sections of CIPA unconstitutional for requiring librarians to violate adult patrons' First Amendment rights to free access of information. The Justice Department appealed the ruling to the Supreme Court—i.e., applied for *certiorari*—in September of 2002.

Ashcroft v. Free Speech Coalition, No. 00-795, Slip op. (April 16, 2002) Declared CPPA unconstitutional because (1) it was overbroad, banning more images than it intended, and (2) such computer-generated images (or images involving adults pretending to be children) were not linked to the child abuse that motivated the legal objection to child pornography.

Ashcroft v. American Civil Liberties Union (ACLU), No. 00-1293, Slip op. (May 13, 2002) COPA was declared unconstitutional by the Third Circuit Court of Appeals because its reliance on "contemporary community standards" made it too broad for a medium that distributed information on a national scale. The Supreme Court, which reviewed the case on the government's appeal of that decision, disagreed and sent *Ashcroft* back to the Third Circuit for consideration of First Amendment issues. Per order of the Court, COPA cannot be enforced at least until a final decision is made.

Concepts and Standards

the Establishment Clause

speech act

protected speech

marketplace of ideas

tyranny of the majority

chilling effect

content restrictions

time, place, and manner restrictions

campus speech code movement

fair notice

hate speech

culture of hatred

actual malice

fighting words

hate crime

political speech

clear and present danger

the Brandenburg standard

imminent lawless action

prior restraint

gag order

shield laws

worthwhile/worthless speech

obscenity, decency, and pornography

contemporary community standards

prurient interest

artistic merit

the Miller standard

the SLAPS test

Beginning Legal Research

The goal of POINT/COUNTERPOINT is not only to provide the reader with an introduction to a controversial issue affecting society, but also to encourage the reader to explore the issue more fully. This appendix, then, is meant to serve as a guide to the reader in researching the current state of the law as well as exploring some of the public-policy arguments as to why existing laws should be changed or new laws are needed.

Like many types of research, legal research has become much faster and more accessible with the invention of the Internet. This appendix discusses some of the best starting points, but of course "surfing the Net" will uncover endless additional sources of information—some more reliable than others. Some important sources of law are not yet available on the Internet, but these can generally be found at the larger public and university libraries. Librarians usually are happy to point patrons in the right direction.

The most important source of law in the United States is the Constitution. Originally enacted in 1787, the Constitution outlines the structure of our federal government and sets limits on the types of laws that the federal government and state governments can pass. Through the centuries, a number of amendments have been added to or changed in the Constitution, most notably the first ten amendments, known collectively as the Bill of Rights, which guarantee important civil liberties. Each state also has its own constitution, many of which are similar to the U.S. Constitution. It is important to be familiar with the U.S. Constitution because so many of our laws are affected by its requirements. State constitutions often provide protections of individual rights that are even stronger than those set forth in the U.S. Constitution.

Within the guidelines of the U.S. Constitution, Congress—both the House of Representatives and the Senate—passes bills that are either vetoed or signed into law by the President. After the passage of the law, it becomes part of the United States Code, which is the official compilation of federal laws. The state legislatures use a similar process, in which bills become law when signed by the state's governor. Each state has its own official set of laws, some of which are published by the state and some of which are published by commercial publishers. The U.S. Code and the state codes are an important source of legal research; generally, legislators make efforts to make the language of the law as clear as possible.

However, reading the text of a federal or state law generally provides only part of the picture. In the American system of government, after the legislature passes laws and the executive (U.S. President or state governor) signs them, it is up to the judicial branch of the government, the court system, to interpret the laws and decide whether they violate any provision of the Constitution. At the state level, each state's supreme court has the ultimate authority in determining what a law means and whether or not it violates the state constitution. However, the federal courts—headed by the U.S. Supreme Court—can review state laws and court decisions to determine whether they violate federal laws or the U.S. Constitution. For example, a state court may find that a particular criminal law is valid under the state's constitution, but a federal court may then review the state court's decision and determine that the law is invalid under the U.S. Constitution.

It is important, then, to read court decisions when doing legal research. The Constitution uses language that is intentionally very general—for example, prohibiting "unreasonable searches and seizures" by the police—and court cases often provide more guidance. For example, the U.S. Supreme Court's 2001 decision in *Kyllo v. United States* held that scanning the outside of a person's house using a heat sensor to determine whether the person is growing marijuana is unreasonable—*if* it is done without a search warrant secured from a judge. Supreme Court decisions provide the most definitive explanation of the law of the land, and it is therefore important to include these in research. Often, when the Supreme Court has not decided a case on a particular issue, a decision by a federal appeals court or a state supreme court can provide guidance; but just as laws and constitutions can vary from state to state, so can federal courts be split on a particular interpretation of federal law or the U.S. Constitution. For example, federal appeals courts in Louisiana and California may reach opposite conclusions in similar cases.

Lawyers and courts refer to statutes and court decisions through a formal system of citations. Use of these citations reveals which court made the decision (or which legislature passed the statute) and when and enables the reader to locate the statute or court case quickly in a law library. For example, the legendary Supreme Court case *Brown v. Board of Education* has the legal citation 347 U.S. 483 (1954). At a law library, this 1954 decision can be found on page 483 of volume 347 of the U.S. Reports, the official collection of the Supreme Court's decisions. Citations can also be helpful in locating court cases on the Internet.

Understanding the current state of the law leads only to a partial understanding of the issues covered by the POINT/COUNTERPOINT series. For a fuller understanding of the issues, it is necessary to look at public-policy arguments that the current state of the law is not adequately addressing the issue. Many groups lobby for new legislation or changes to existing legislation; the National Rifle Association (NRA), for example, lobbies Congress and the state legislatures constantly to make existing gun control laws less restrictive and not to pass additional laws. The NRA and other groups dedicated to various causes might also intervene in pending court cases: a group such as Planned Parenthood might file a brief *amicus curiae* (as "a friend of the court")—called an "amicus brief"—in a lawsuit that could affect abortion rights. Interest groups also use the media to influence public opinion, issuing press releases and frequently appearing in interviews on news programs and talk shows. The books in POINT/COUNTERPOINT list some of the interest groups that are active in the issue at hand, but in each case there are countless other groups working at the local, state, and national levels. It is important to read everything with a critical eye, for sometimes interest groups present information in a way that can be read only to their advantage. The informed reader must always look for bias.

Finding sources of legal information on the Internet is relatively simple thanks to "portal" sites such as FindLaw (*www.findlaw.com*), which provides access to a variety of constitutions, statutes, court opinions, law review articles, news articles, and other resources—including all Supreme Court decisions issued since 1893. Other useful sources of information include the U.S. Government Printing Office (*www.gpo.gov*), which contains a complete copy of the U.S. Code, and the Library of Congress's THOMAS system (*thomas.loc.gov*), which offers access to bills pending before Congress as well as recently passed laws. Of course, the Internet changes every second of every day, so it is best to do some independent searching. Most cases, studies, and opinions that are cited or referred to in public debate can be found online—and *everything* can be found in one library or another.

The Internet can provide a basic understanding of most important legal issues, but not all sources can be found there. To find some documents it is necessary to visit the law library of a university or a public law library; some cities have public law libraries, and many library systems keep legal documents at the main branch. On the following page are some common citation forms.

COMMON CITATION FORMS

Source of Law	Sample Citation	Notes
U.S. Supreme Court	*Employment Division v. Smith*, 485 U.S. 660 (1988)	The U.S. Reports is the official record of Supreme Court decisions. There is also an unofficial Supreme Court ("S.Ct.") reporter.
U.S. Court of Appeals	*United States v. Lambert*, 695 F.2d 536 (11th Cir.1983)	Appellate cases appear in the Federal Reporter, designated by "F." The 11th Circuit has jurisdiction in Alabama, Florida, and Georgia.
U.S. District Court	*Carillon Importers, Ltd. v. Frank Pesce Group, Inc.*, 913 F.Supp. 1559 (S.D.Fla.1996)	Federal trial-level decisions are reported in the Federal Supplement ("F.Supp."). Some states have multiple federal districts; this case originated in the Southern District of Florida.
U.S. Code	Thomas Jefferson Commemoration Commission Act, 36 U.S.C., §149 (2002)	Sometimes the popular names of legislation—names with which the public may be familiar—are included with the U.S. Code citation.
State Supreme Court	*Sterling v. Cupp*, 290 Ore. 611, 614, 625 P.2d 123, 126 (1981)	The Oregon Supreme Court decision is reported in both the state's reporter and the Pacific regional reporter.
State statute	Pennsylvania Abortion Control Act of 1982, 18 Pa. Cons. Stat. 3203-3220 (1990)	States use many different citation formats for their statutes.

107

ALAN ALLPORT was born in Whiston, England, and grew up in East Yorkshire. He holds a master's degree in history from the University of Pennsylvania and is now a Ph.D. candidate at that institution, with a special interest in European history of the 19th and 20th centuries. He is currently working on projects connected to the social and cultural histories of the two world wars. He lives in Philadelphia.

ALAN MARZILLI, of Durham, North Carolina, is an independent consultant working on several ongoing projects for state and federal government agencies and nonprofit organizations. He has spoken about mental health issues in over twenty states, the District of Columbia, and Puerto Rico; his work includes training mental health administrators, nonprofit management and staff, and people with mental illness and their family members on a wide variety of topics, including effective advocacy, community-based mental health services, and housing. He has written several handbooks and training curricula that are used nationally. He managed statewide and national mental health advocacy programs and worked for several public interest lobbying organizations in Washington, D.C. while studying law at Georgetown University.